WILD
FLOWERS

IN CROSS-STITCH

WILD FLOWERS

IN CROSS-STITCH

Charted Designs By

JULIE S. HASLER

BLANDFORD

Colour photography by
James Mayer of cross-stitch
embroidery by Joyce Freel

First published in the UK 1989 by Blandford Press,
an imprint of Cassell plc
Artillery House, Artillery Row, London SW1P 1RT
Reprinted 1990

Distributed in the United States by
Sterling Publishing Co, Inc,
387 Park Avenue South, New York, NY 10016

Distributed in Australia by
Capricorn Link (Australia) Pty Ltd
PO Box 665, Lane Cove, NSW 2066

British Library Cataloguing in Publication Data
Hasler, Julie S.
  Wild flowers in cross-stitch : charted
  designs.
  1.   Embroidery. Cross-stitch – Patterns
  I.   Title
  746.44

ISBN 0 7137 2005 0 (Paperback)
ISBN 0 7137 2218 5 (Hardback)

Typeset by Inforum Ltd, Portsmouth
Printed in Great Britain by Alden Press, Oxford

4

Contents

Preface

The favourite stitch of our great-grandmothers, cross-stitch is becoming increasingly popular in these modern times for the decoration of household furnishings, linen, children's clothes, in fact anything which lends itself to this type of embroidery. The possibilities are endless.

Cross-stitch is one of the simplest, most versatile and elegant needlecrafts, and examples of its use can be found in many different countries and different eras.

The projects in this book make beautiful gifts for family and friends: gifts with a personal touch which have taken time and care to create, which will still be treasured long after shop-bought gifts have been forgotten.

The designs in this book can be worked by following the charts exactly, or, by using your imagination, you can create your own designs by the use of alternative colours or by combining different motifs from several charts to create embroideries which are uniquely yours.

General directions

The designs in this book are created for counted cross-stitch, a very enjoyable craft which you will find easy to learn and inexpensive as well!

The fabric you choose to sew your designs on and the number of strands of silk you use is your choice.

You will find that the fabric is available in varying thread counts, and that there is a very wide choice of colours: white, ecru, pink, blue, lemon and pale green, to name but a few.

I chose 11-count cotton aida in ecru to sew the designs in this book, using three strands of embroidery cotton for the cross-stitch. Why not use your imagination and choose a fabric colour that will enhance your embroidery?

The charts are easy to read. Each square on the chart represents one stitch to be taken on the fabric and each different symbol represents a different colour, the empty squares being background fabric.

A colour key is given with each design.

If you wish to decorate clothing with any of the designs in this book, the most satisfactory method is to work the design over cross-stitch fabric basted to the clothing material and remove the cross-stitch fabric afterwards, thread by thread. This will leave the cross-stitch embroidery on the clothing material beneath.

Relax, enjoy sewing the designs, and make something beautiful for you and your home.

Techniques

Cross-stitch

To begin: bring the thread through at the lower right-hand side, leaving a short length of thread on the underside of the work and anchoring it with the first few stitches as in Diagrams 1 and 2. Insert the needle across the mesh into the next hole above and diagonally to the left and bring it out through the hole across the mesh but immediately below. Half the stitch is now completed.

Continue in the same way to the end of the row. Complete the upper half of the stitch by returning in the opposite direction, as shown in Diagram 3.

Cross-stitch can be worked in either direction, from right to left or left to right, but it is of the utmost importance that the upper half of each cross lies in the same direction.

Backstitch

Backstitch is used in many of the designs, mainly for outlines and finer details.

It is worked from hole to hole and can be stitched as a horizontal, diagonal or vertical line, as shown in Diagram 4.

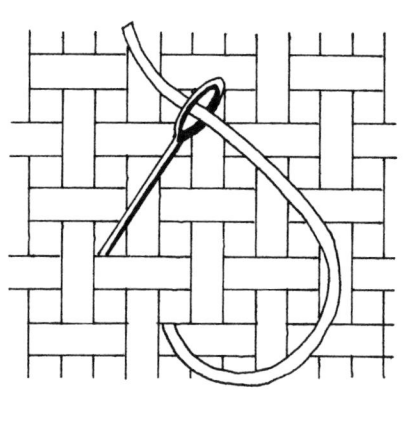

DIAGRAM 1

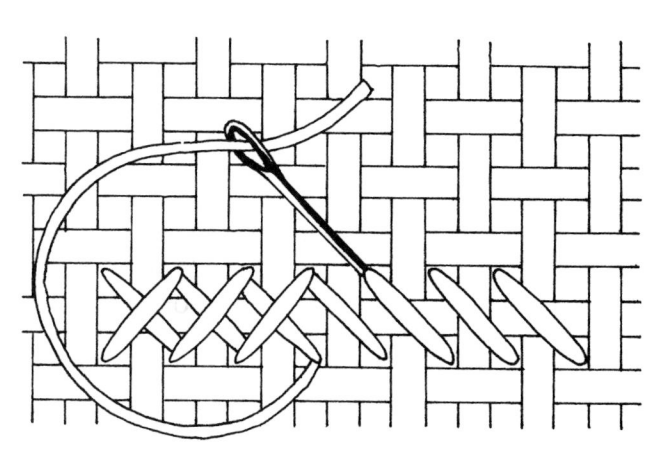

DIAGRAM 3

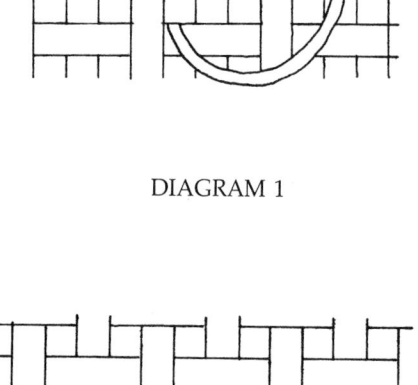

DIAGRAM 2

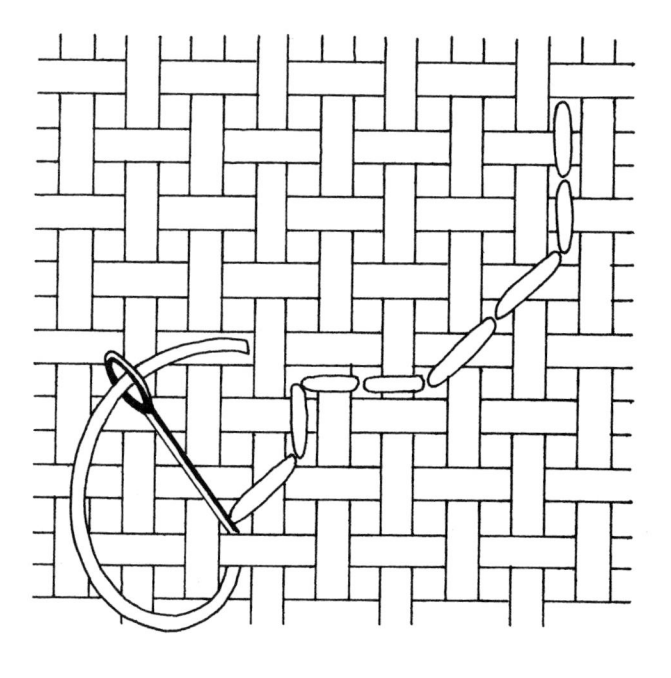

DIAGRAM 4

Materials

1 NEEDLES A small blunt tapestry needle, No. 24 or 26.

2 SCISSORS A sharp pair of embroidery scissors is essential.

3 EMBROIDERY HOOP A round, plastic or wooden hoop with a screw-type tension adjuster, 4 inches, 5 inches or 6 inches in diameter, is ideal for cross-stitch. Place the area of fabric to be embroidered over the inner ring and gently push the outer ring over it, ensuring that the fabric is taut and the mesh straight.

4 THREADS DMC six-strand embroidery cotton has been used to colour-code the designs in this book. The number of strands used will depend on the fabric you decide to work on.

5 FABRIC Do not use a fabric which does not have an even weave, as this will distort the embroidery either vertically or horizontally. An evenweave fabric on which it is easy to count the threads should be used. There are a few to choose from in varying thread counts. The most popular fabrics used are aida cloth, linen and hardanger cloth.
Cotton aida is available in the following sizes: 8, 11, 14 and 18 threads-per-inch.
Linen is available in the following sizes: 19/20, 25/26 and 30/31 threads-per-inch.
Hardanger is 22 threads-per-inch.

Preparing to work

To determine the size of the finished embroidery, count the squares on the chart for the entire width and depth of the design, and divide each by the number of threads-per-inch in the fabric you intend to use. This will give the dimensions in inches. Cut the fabric at least 2 inches wider each way than the finished size to allow for finishing. To prevent the fabric fraying, either machine-stitch or whip-stitch the outer edges or alternatively bind them with masking tape.

Find the centre of the fabric by folding it in half vertically and then horizontally. Mark the centre with a line of basting stitches both lengthwise and widthwise. Many of the charts in this book have arrows marking the vertical and horizontal centres. Follow these arrows to their intersection to locate the centre of the chart.

It is preferable to begin cross-stitch at the top of the design. To find the top, count the squares up from the centre of the chart and then the number of holes up from the centre of the fabric. Ensure that the fabric is held tautly in the embroidery hoop, as this makes stitching easier, enabling the needle to be pushed through the holes without piercing the fibres of the fabric.

If the fabric loosens while working, retighten as necessary. When working with stranded cotton, always separate the strands before threading the needle. This will give better coverage of the fabric.

The number of strands will depend on the fabric count that you use.

Finishing

When the embroidery is finished, it will need to be pressed. Place the finished work right side down on your ironing board, cover it with a thin, slightly dampened cloth, and iron.

If you intend to frame the finished embroidery yourself, you will need to block it. Cut a piece of board to the desired size and place the finished embroidery over it. Fold the surplus fabric to the back and secure along the top edge of the board with pins. Pull firmly over the opposite edge and pin in position.

Repeat along both side edges, pulling the fabric until it is lying taut on the board.

Secure at the back by lacing from side to side on all four sides with a strong thread. Remove the pins and frame as desired.

Wild flower patterns

The following pages contain twenty wild flower designs
which can be sewn as wall-hangings, pictures, chairbacks
or many other things to brighten up your home.

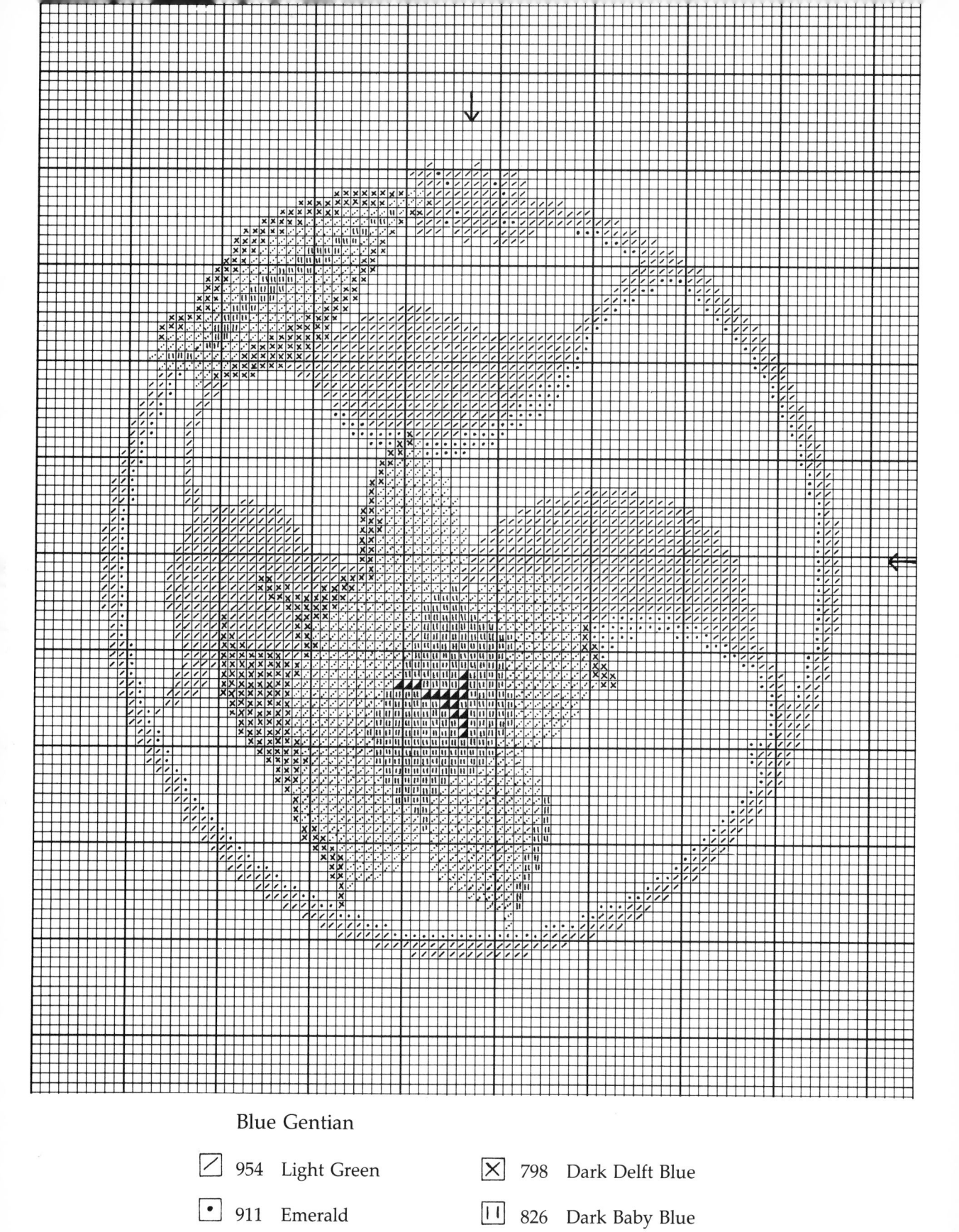

Blue Gentian

/	954	Light Green	✗	798	Dark Delft Blue
•	911	Emerald	‖	826	Dark Baby Blue
∴	827	Light Baby Blue	◢	—	White

15

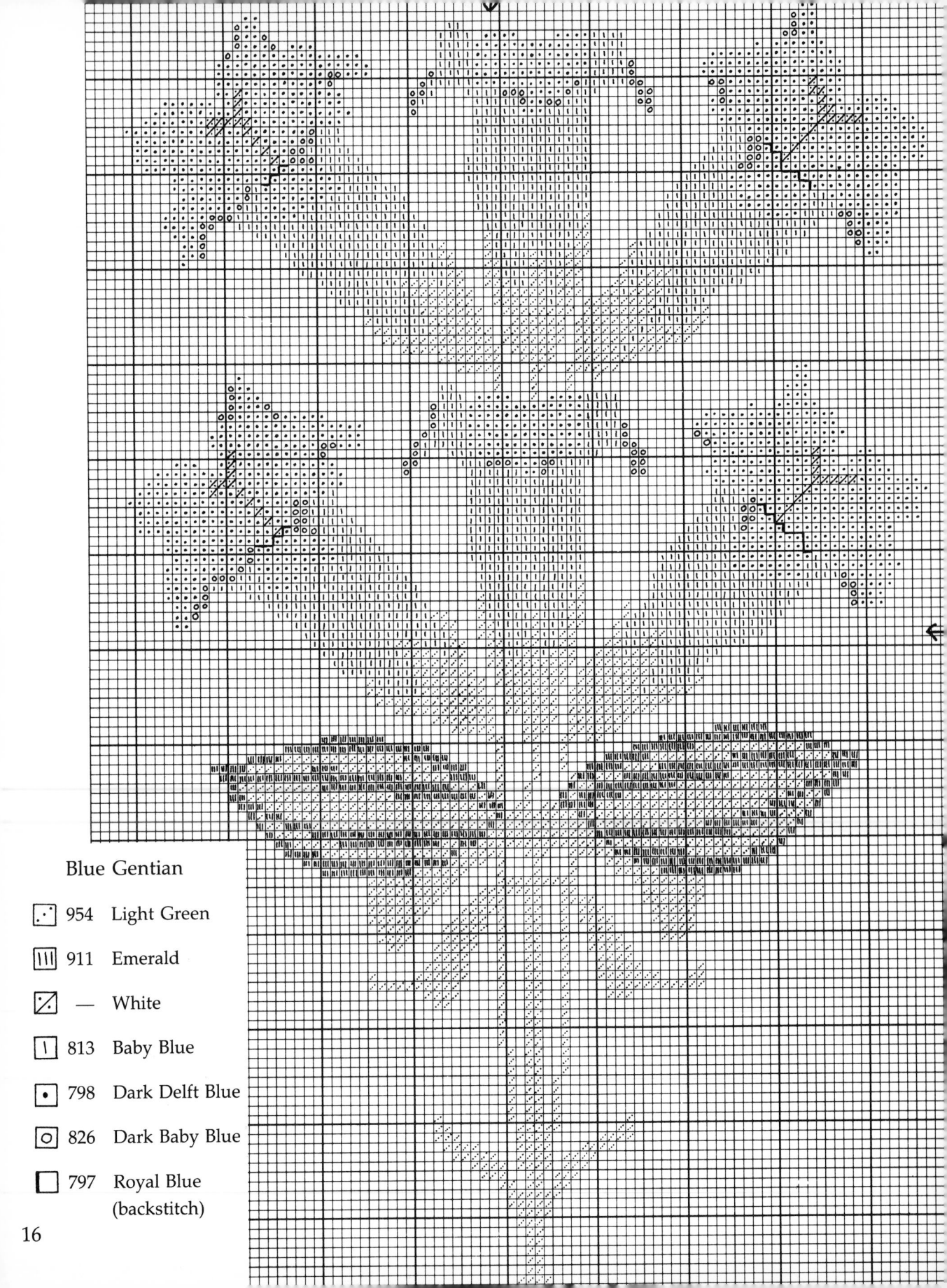

Blue Gentian

Symbol	Code	Color
⊡	954	Light Green
⦀	911	Emerald
◿	—	White
＼	813	Baby Blue
●	798	Dark Delft Blue
○	826	Dark Baby Blue
☐	797	Royal Blue (backstitch)

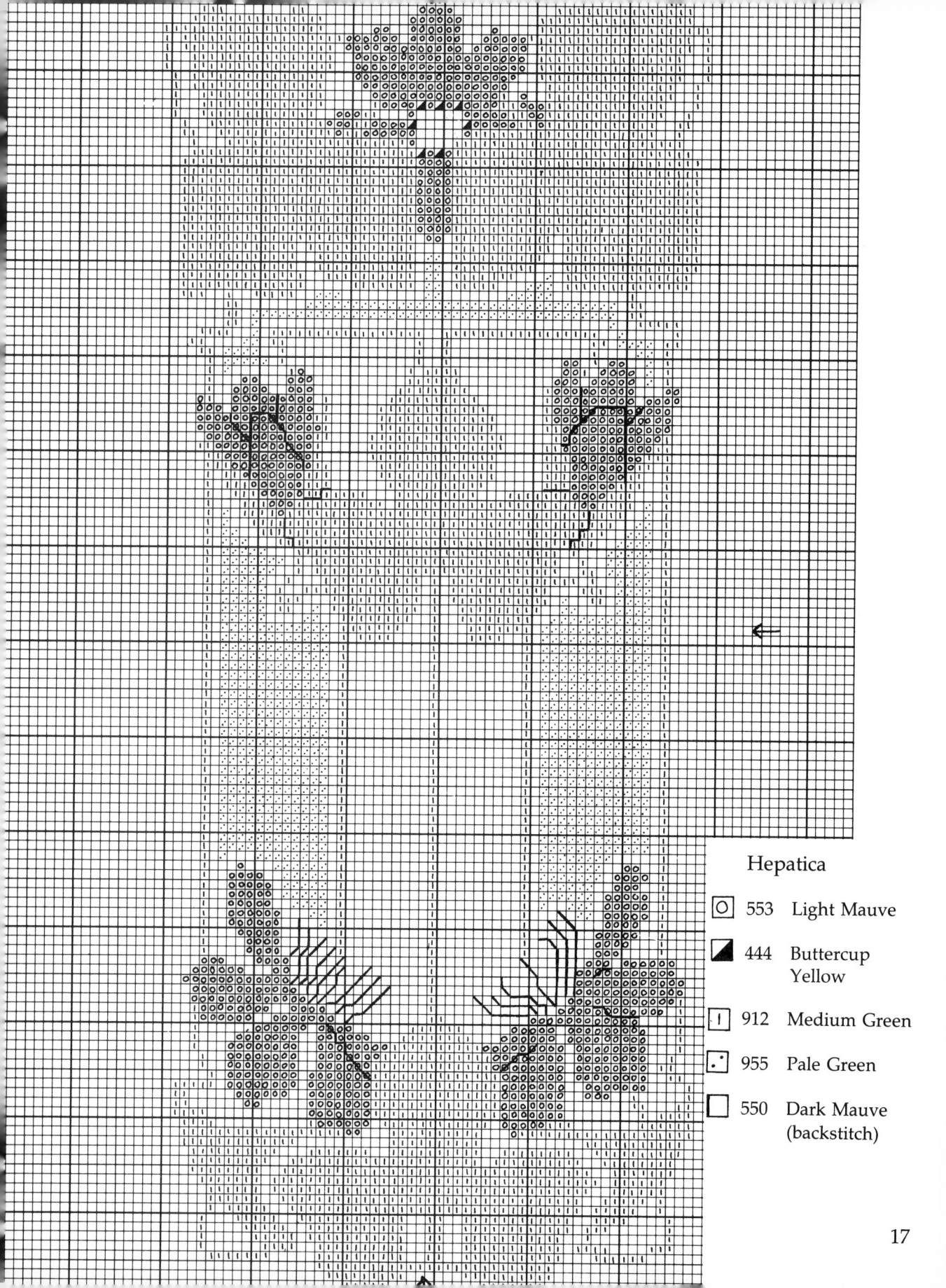

Hepatica

⊙	553	Light Mauve
◢	444	Buttercup Yellow
I	912	Medium Green
∴	955	Pale Green
☐	550	Dark Mauve (backstitch)

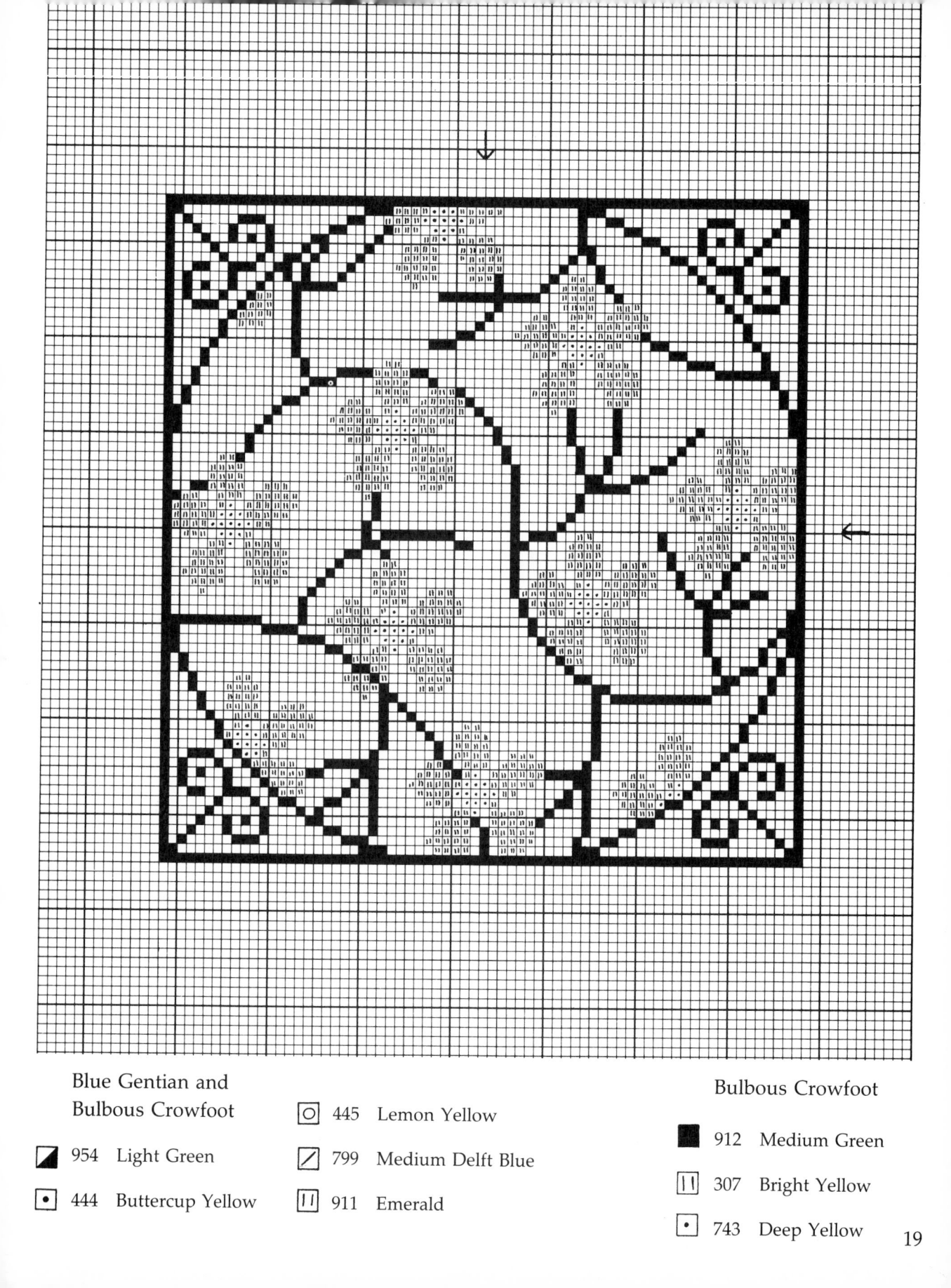

Blue Gentian and
Bulbous Crowfoot

| | 445 | Lemon Yellow |

| | 799 | Medium Delft Blue |

| | 911 | Emerald |

| | 954 | Light Green |

| | 444 | Buttercup Yellow |

Bulbous Crowfoot

| | 912 | Medium Green |

| | 307 | Bright Yellow |

| | 743 | Deep Yellow |

19

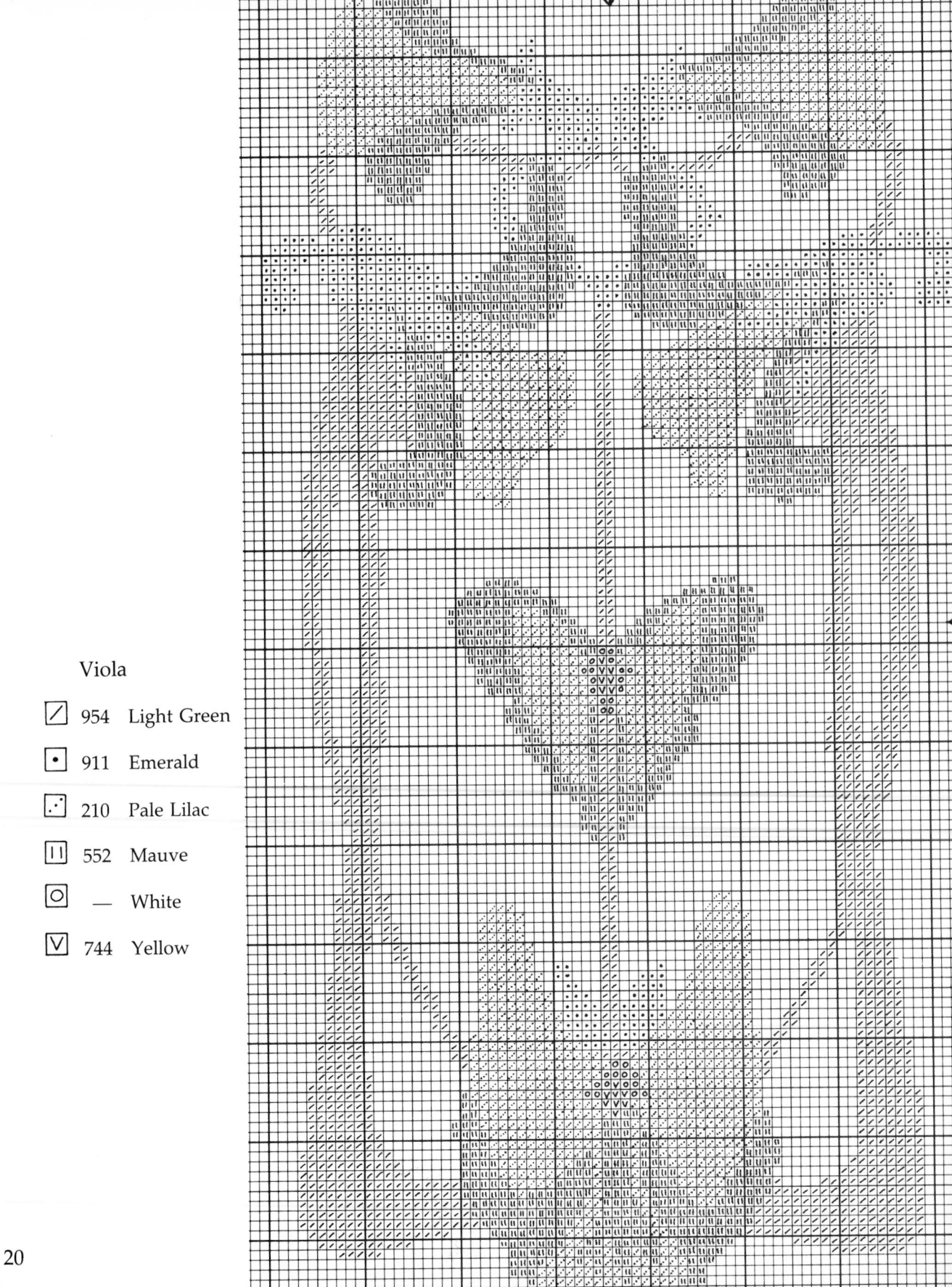

Viola

☑	954	Light Green
•	911	Emerald
⊡	210	Pale Lilac
Ⅱ	552	Mauve
⊙	—	White
⒱	744	Yellow

Hepatica

I I	905	Medium Parrot Green	O	552	Mauve
∕	906	Parrot Green	■	444	Buttercup Yellow
•	907	Light Green	.∙	554	Lilac

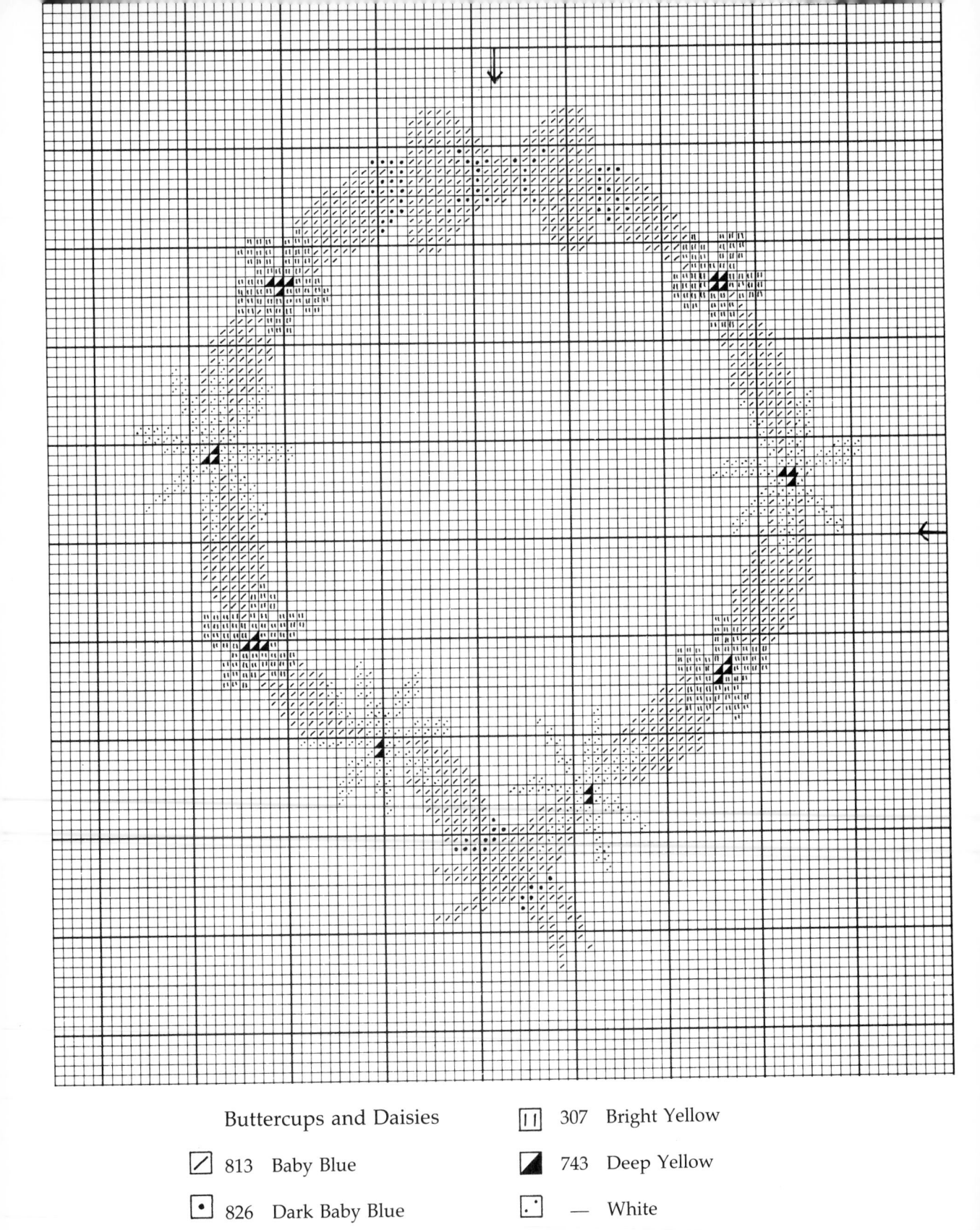

Buttercups and Daisies

⬚	307	Bright Yellow
⟋	813	Baby Blue
◢	743	Deep Yellow
⬚	826	Dark Baby Blue
⬚	—	White

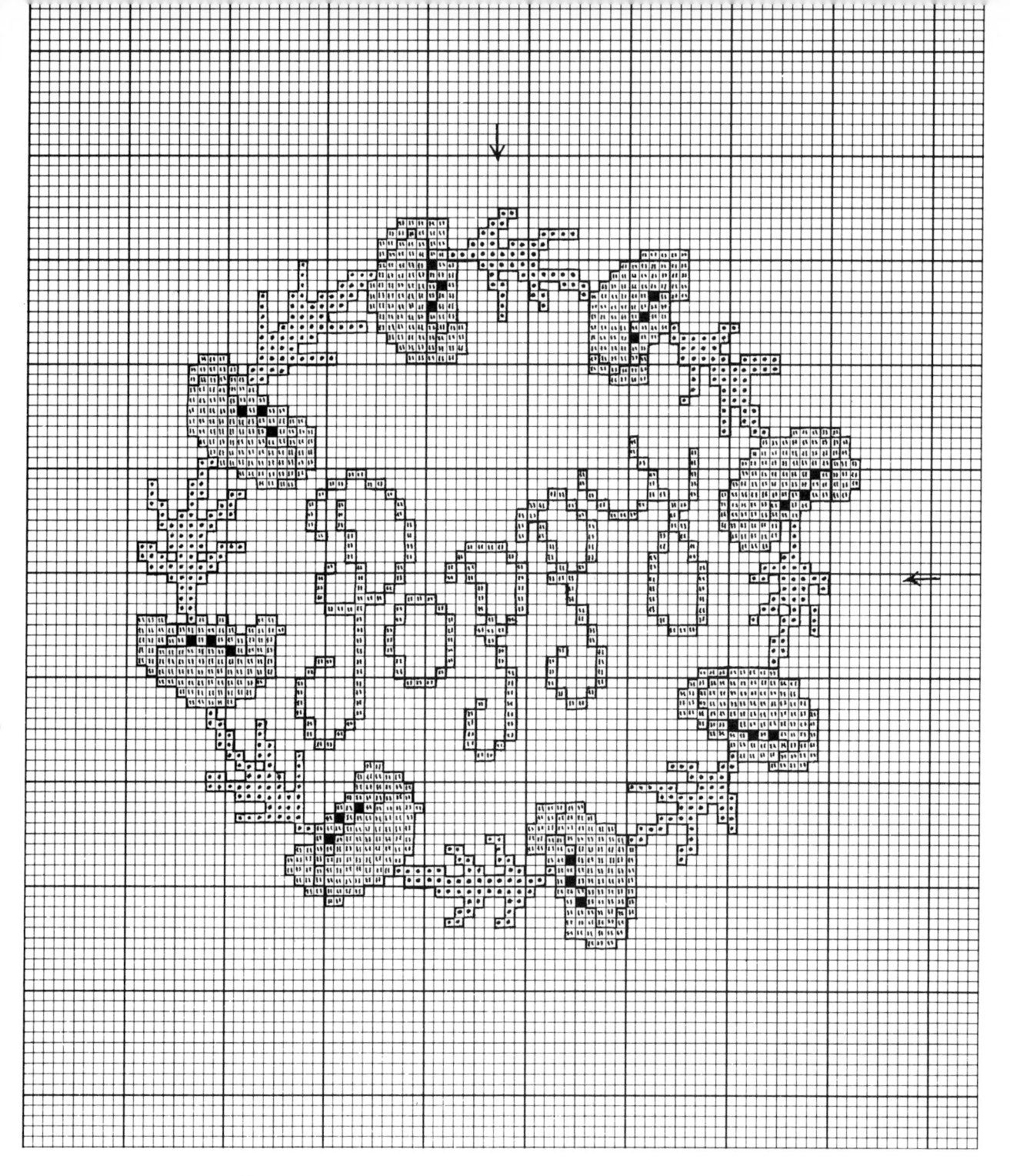

Poppy

- ● 912 Medium Green
- ☐ 321 Poppy Red
- ■ 310 Black
- ☐ 310 Black (backstitch)

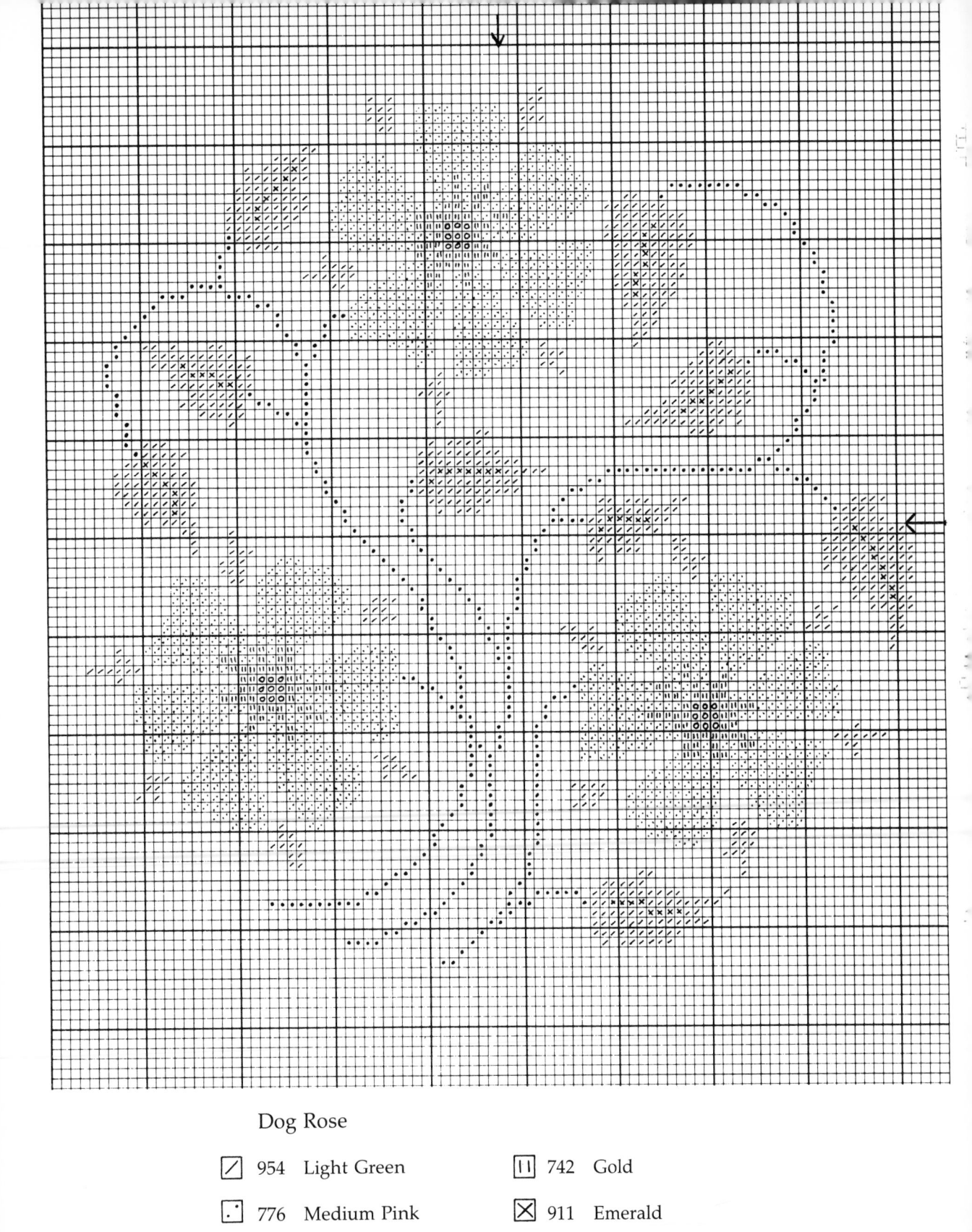

Dog Rose

⟋	954	Light Green	∐	742	Gold
⊡	776	Medium Pink	⊠	911	Emerald
⊙	745	Pale Yellow	⊡	738	Very Light Tan

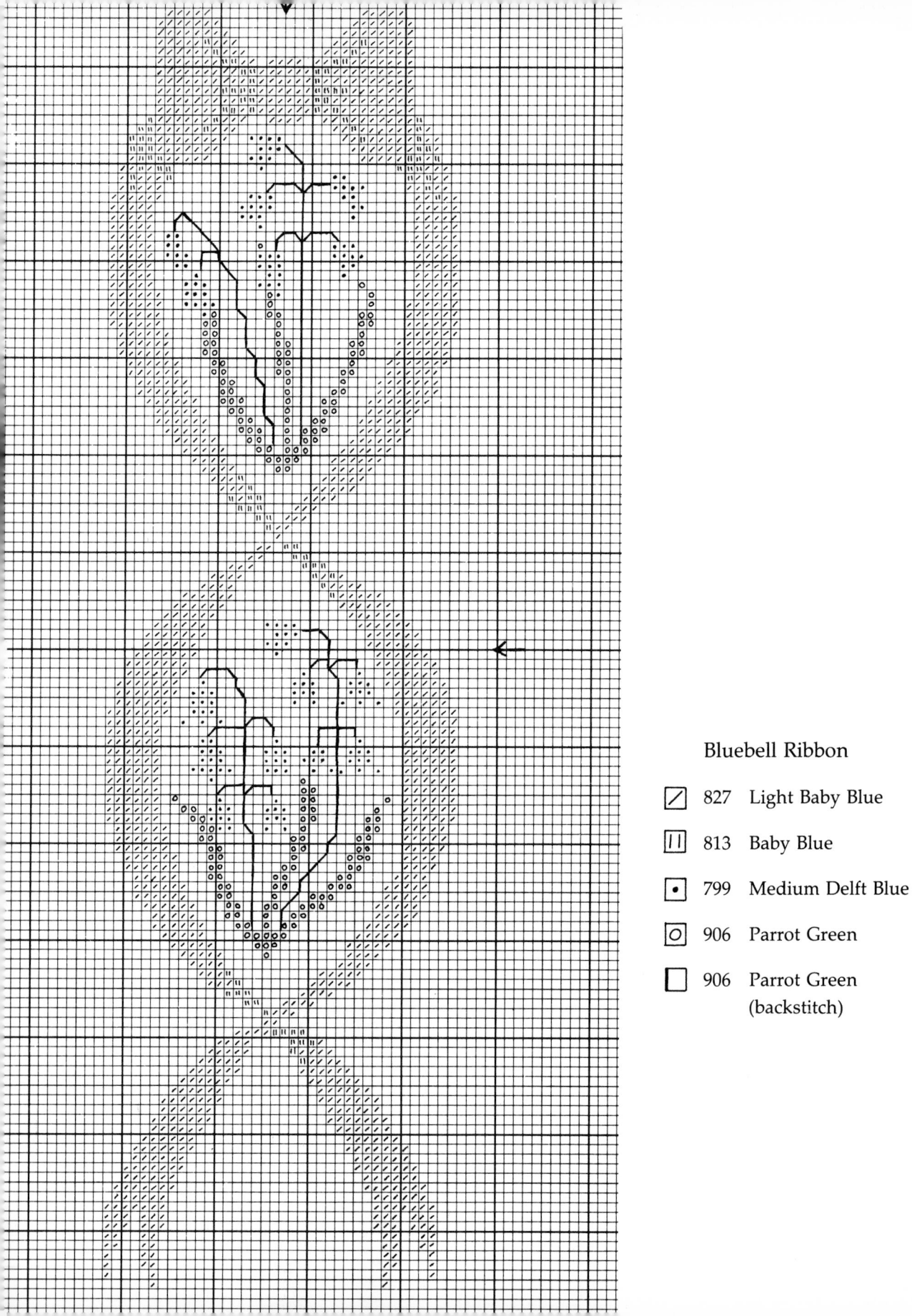

Bluebell Ribbon

⧄	827	Light Baby Blue
‖	813	Baby Blue
•	799	Medium Delft Blue
⊙	906	Parrot Green
☐	906	Parrot Green (backstitch)

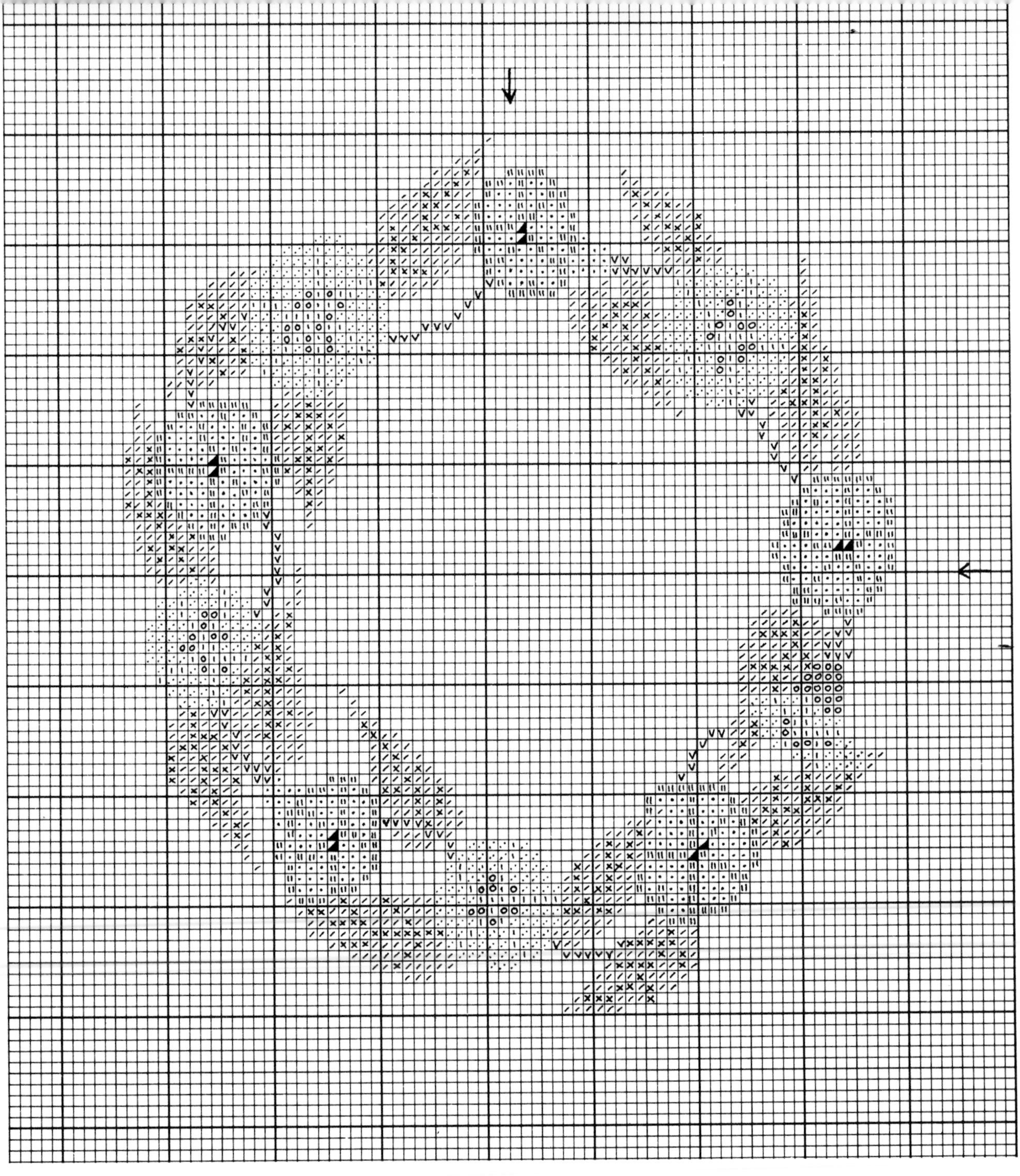

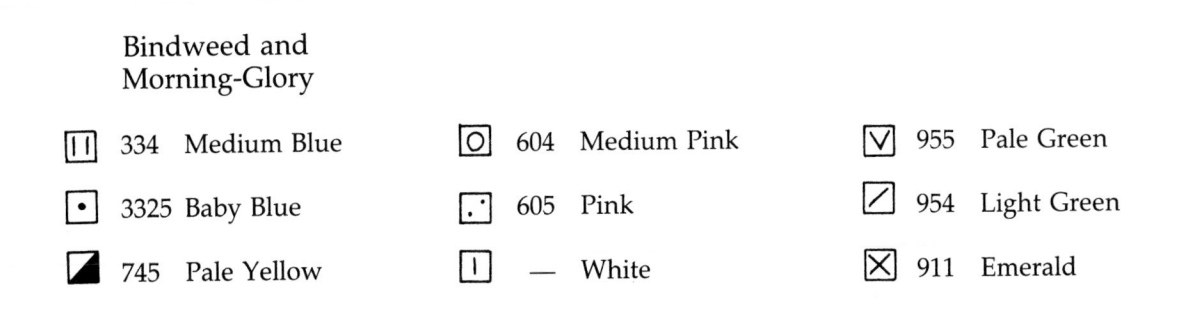

Bindweed and Morning-Glory

⊟	334	Medium Blue	⊡	604	Medium Pink	⊻	955	Pale Green
⊡	3325	Baby Blue	⊡	605	Pink	⧄	954	Light Green
◪	745	Pale Yellow	⊡	—	White	⊠	911	Emerald

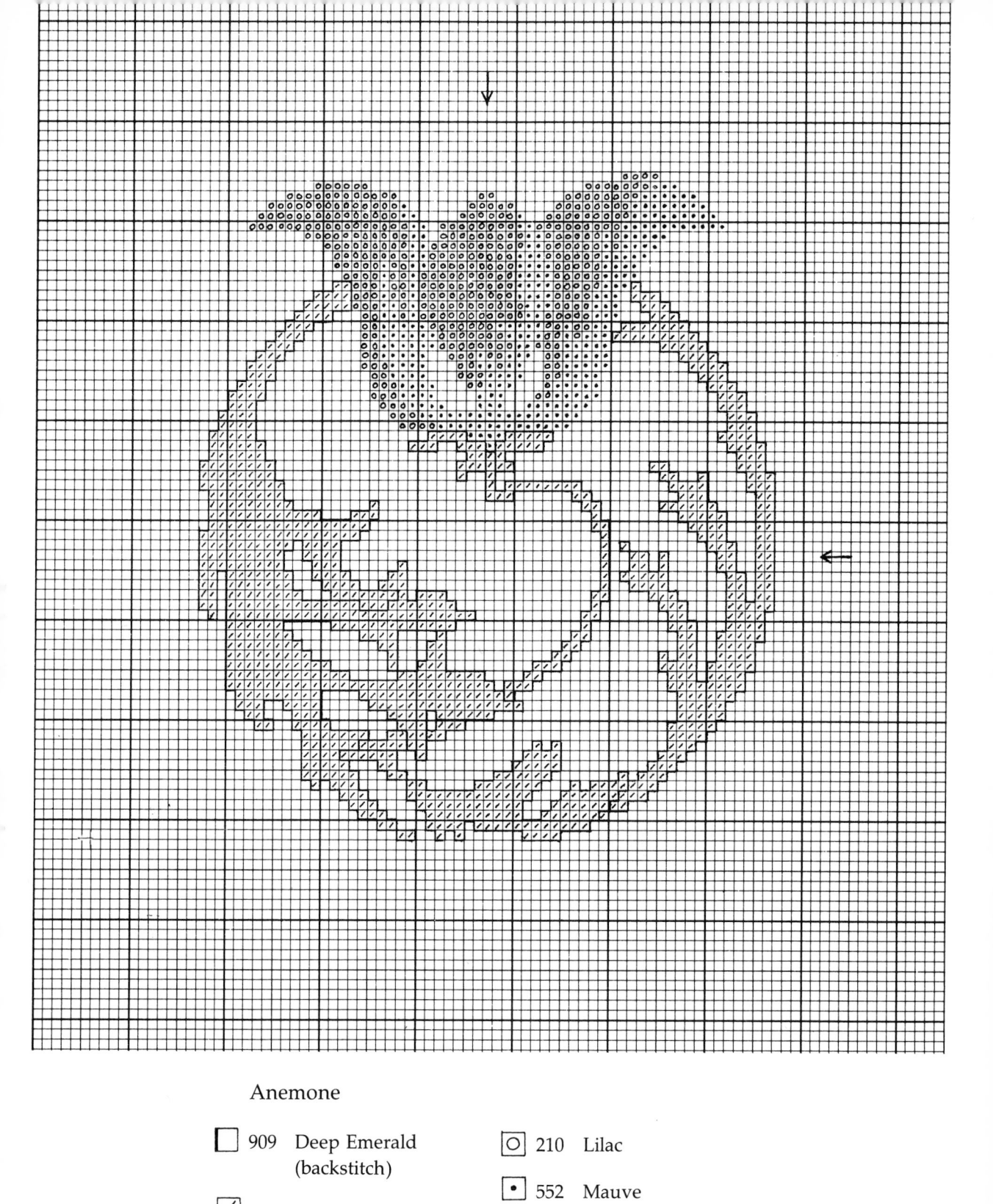

Anemone

| | 909 | Deep Emerald (backstitch) |
| | 955 | Pale Green |

| O | 210 | Lilac |
| • | 552 | Mauve |

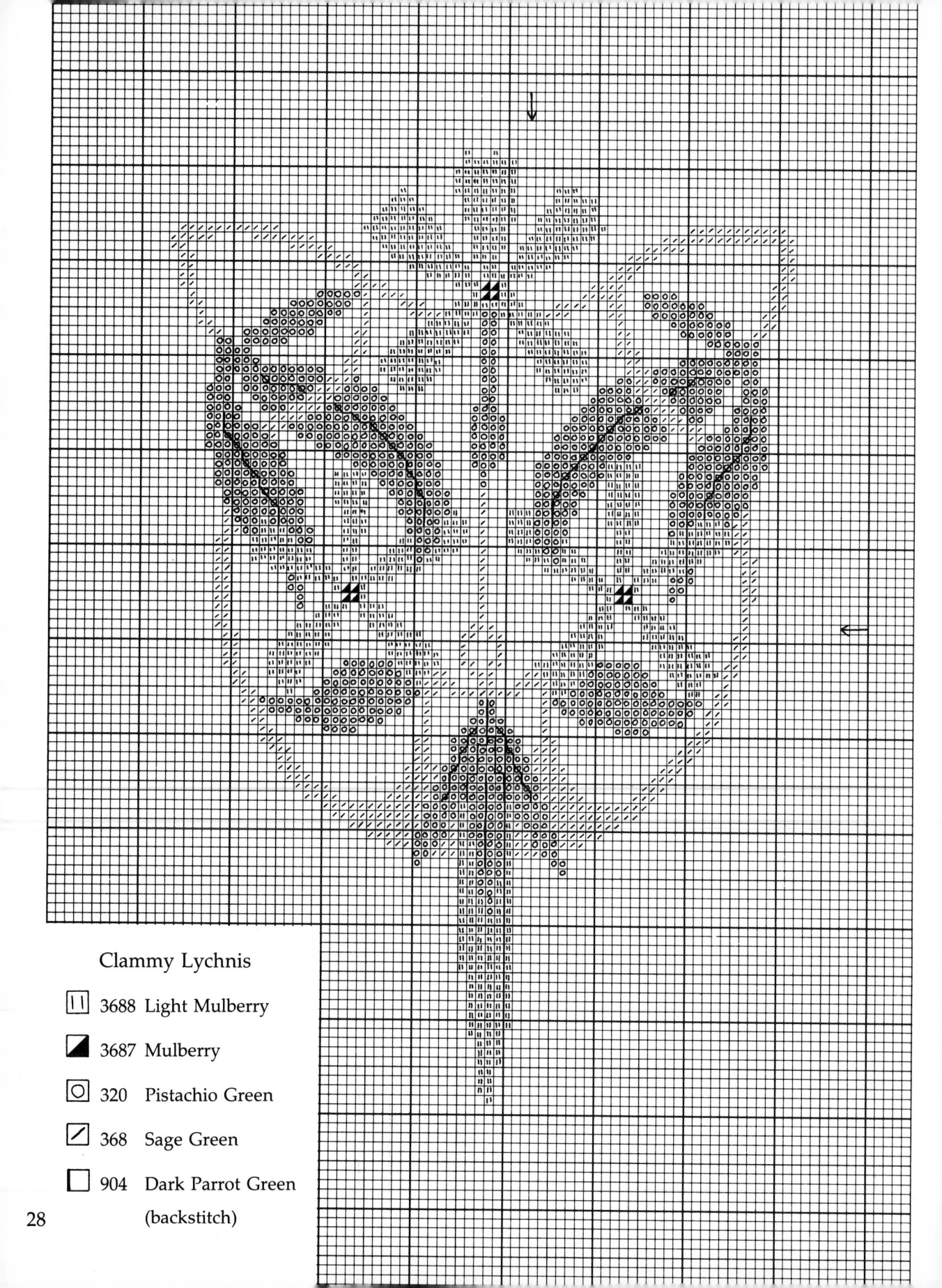

Clammy Lychnis

11	3688 Light Mulberry
◢	3687 Mulberry
O	320 Pistachio Green
⟋	368 Sage Green
☐	904 Dark Parrot Green
	(backstitch)

28

Poppy trio

■	310	Black
•	906	Parrot Green
..	321	Poppy Red
/	498	Deep Red
II	904	Dark Parrot Green

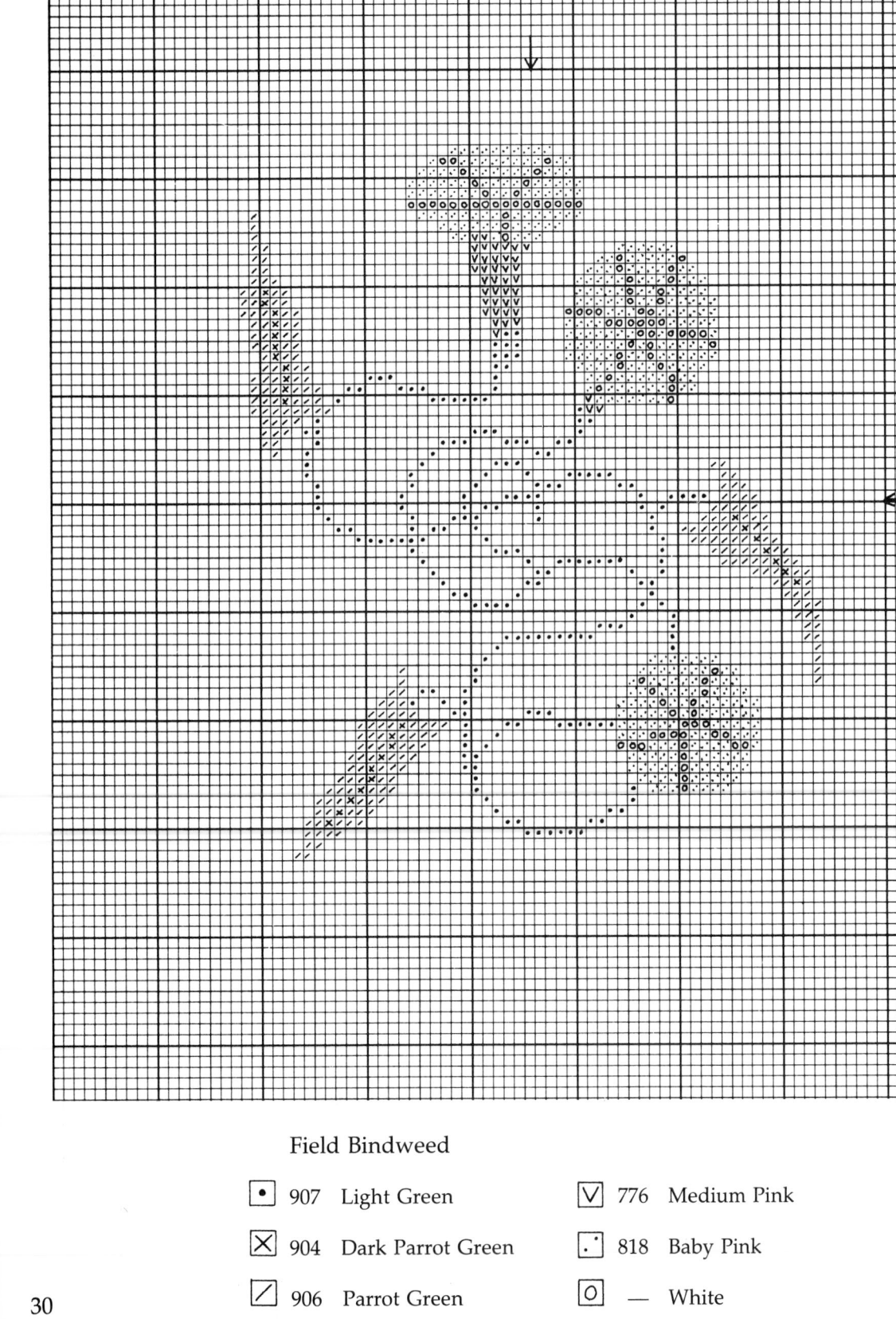

Field Bindweed

●	907	Light Green	V	776	Medium Pink
X	904	Dark Parrot Green	∴	818	Baby Pink
∕	906	Parrot Green	O	—	White

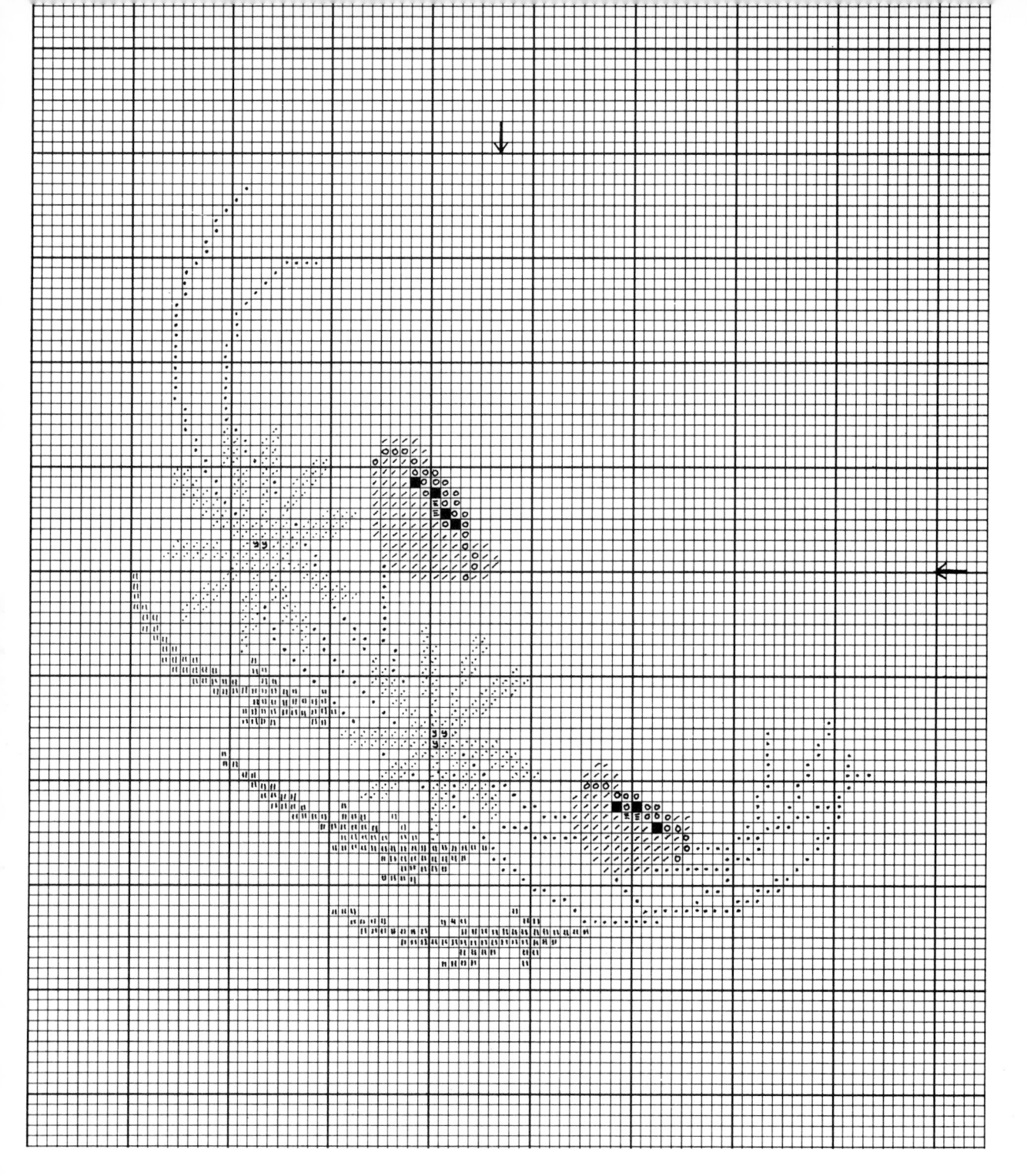

Mixed Flowers pattern

■	310 Black	╱ 321 Poppy Red	ᴜ 444 Buttercup Yellow
◯	815 Deep Red	∥ 905 Medium Parrot Green	• 907 Light Green
☰	318 Medium Grey	⊡ — White	

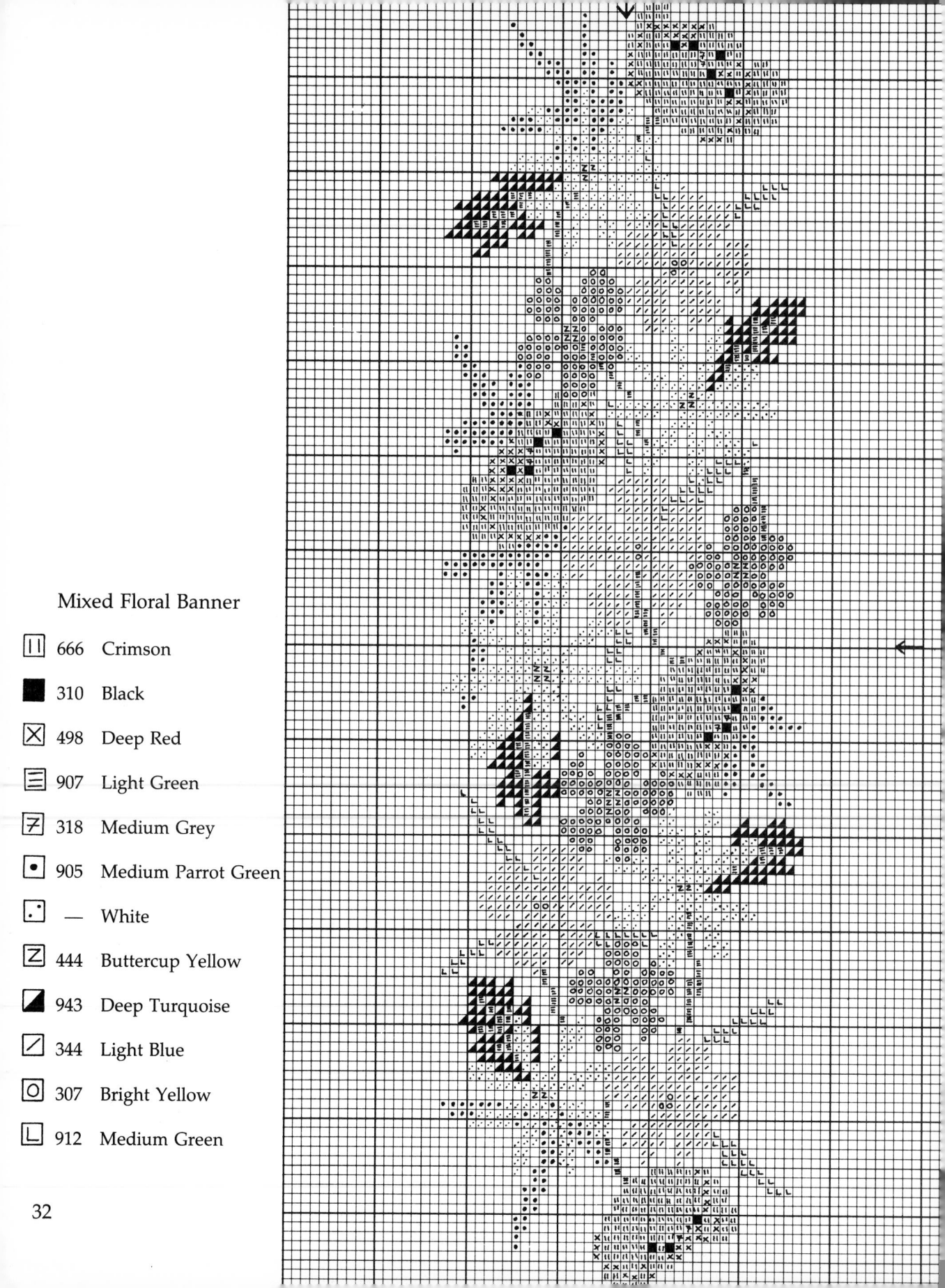

Mixed Floral Banner

Symbol	No.	Colour
ǁ	666	Crimson
■	310	Black
☒	498	Deep Red
☰	907	Light Green
≠	318	Medium Grey
•	905	Medium Parrot Green
⁚	—	White
Z	444	Buttercup Yellow
◪	943	Deep Turquoise
/	344	Light Blue
O	307	Bright Yellow
L	912	Medium Green

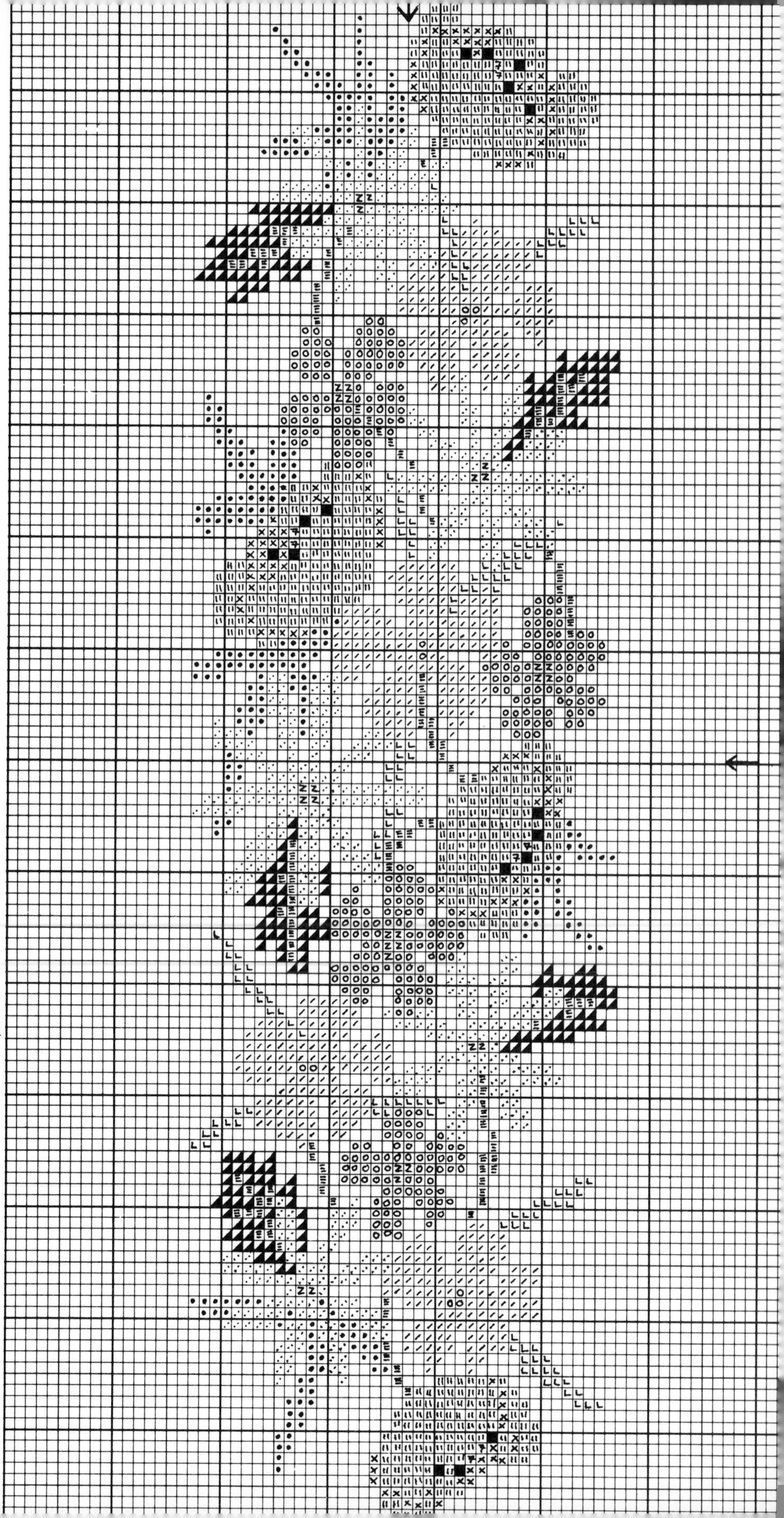

Bearberry

☒	907	Light Green
╱	368	Sage Green
•	895	Dark Forest Green
‖	842	Light Beige-Brown
∴	818	Baby Pink
⊙	3688	Light Mulberry

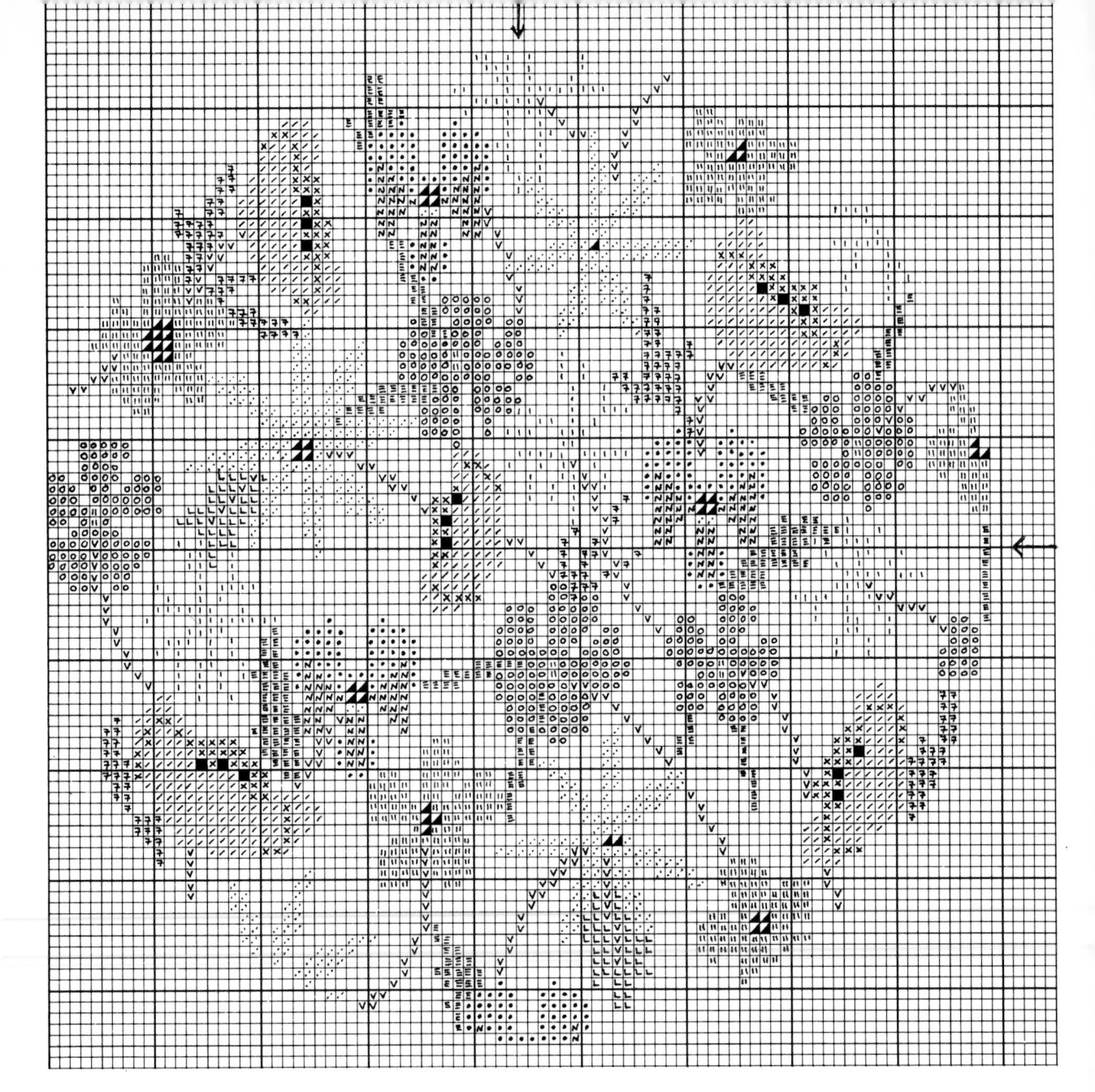

Round Floral Panel Pattern

Symbol	Code	Colour		Symbol	Code	Colour		Symbol	Code	Colour
⊡ —		White		☑	907	Light Green		⊿	666	Crimson
⊡	552	Mauve		Ⓝ	554	Lilac		☒	498	Deep Red
☰	954	Light Green		⊡	605	Pink		⊔	943	Deep Turquoise
⑪	307	Bright Yellow		Ⓞ	813	Light Blue		■	310	Black
◣	444	Buttercup Yellow		⊵	905	Medium Parrot Green				

34

Floral patterns and borders

The designs on the following pages can be used for wall-hangings, pictures and many other household items. The borders will add a distinctive touch to tablecloths, napkin holders, table runners or even bedclothes.

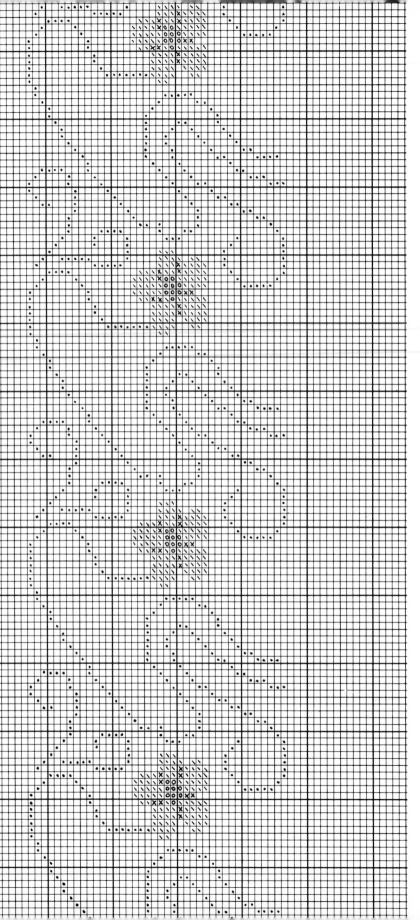

Border:

Bulbous Crowfoot

● 702 Christmas Green

◻ 307 Bright Yellow

⊙ 742 Gold

☒ 444 Buttercup Yellow

Border:

Blue Gentian

$\boxed{\diagdown}$ 799 Medium Delft Blue

$\boxed{II}$ 909 Deep Emerald

$\boxed{\ocircle}$ 912 Medium Green

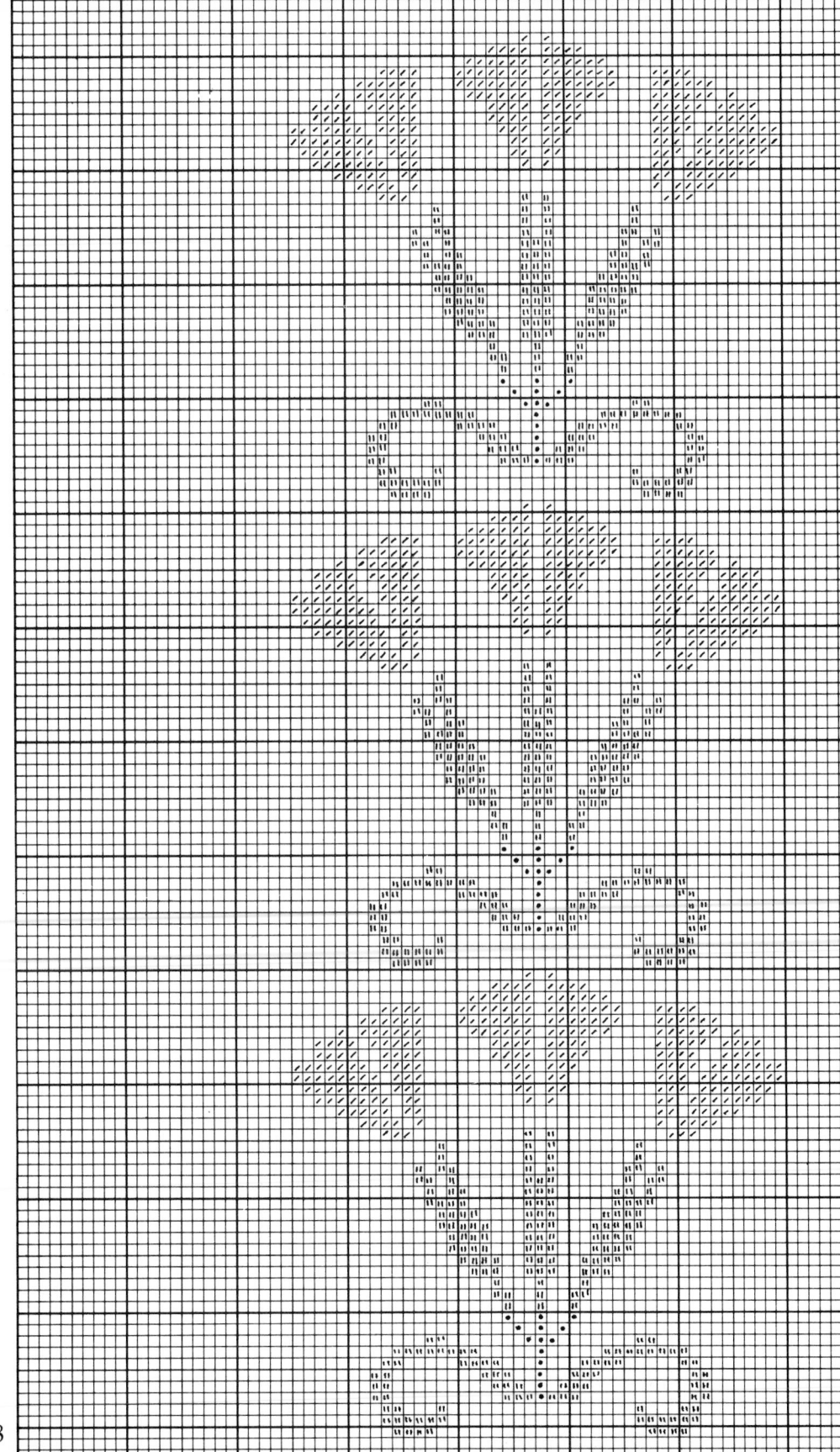

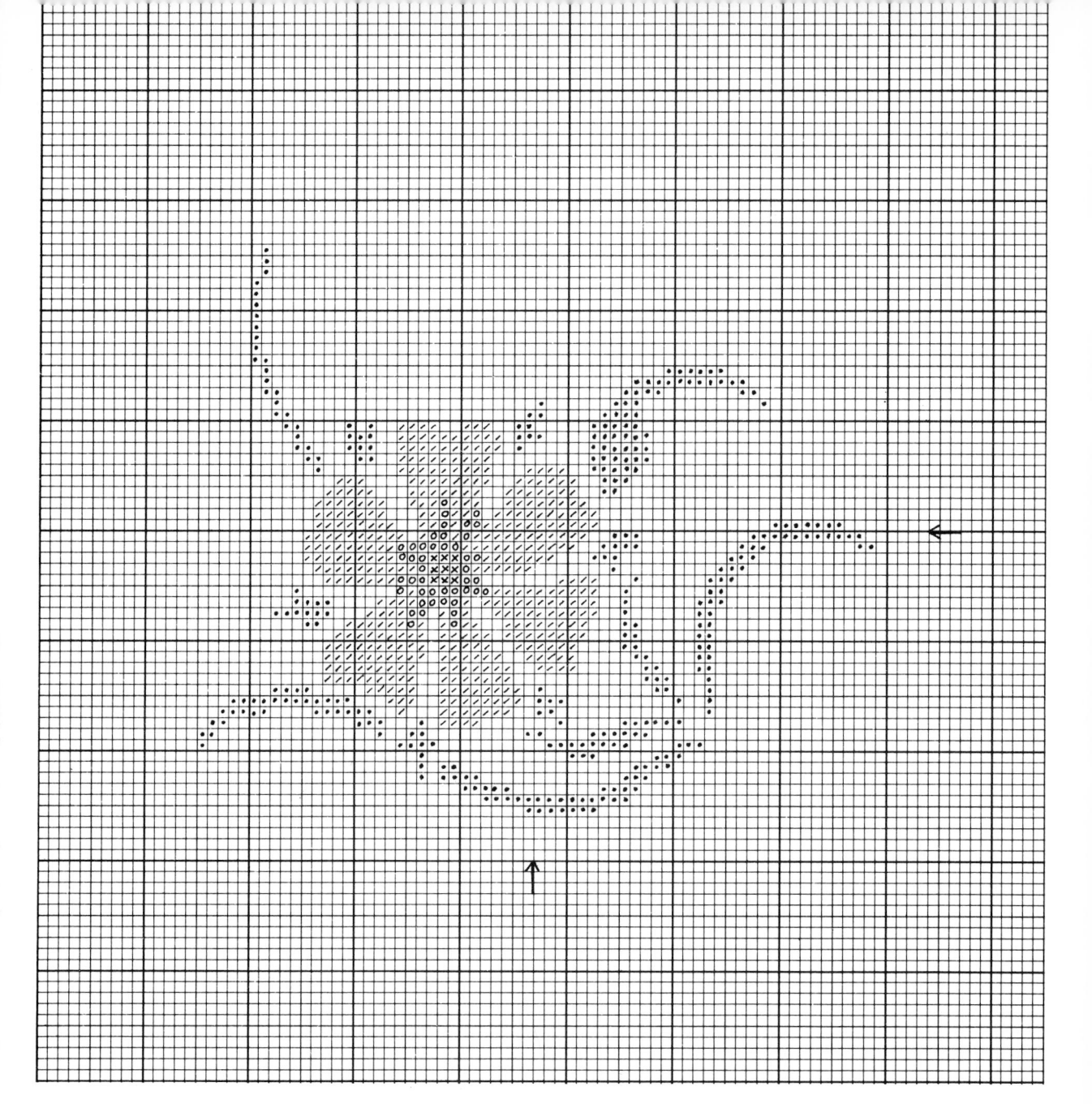

Border: Border Pinks

/ 3688 Light Mulberry

|I| 368 Sage Green

• 320 Pistachio Green

Border: Dog Rose Posy

• 954 Light Green

/ 776 Medium Pink

O 742 Gold

X 744 Yellow

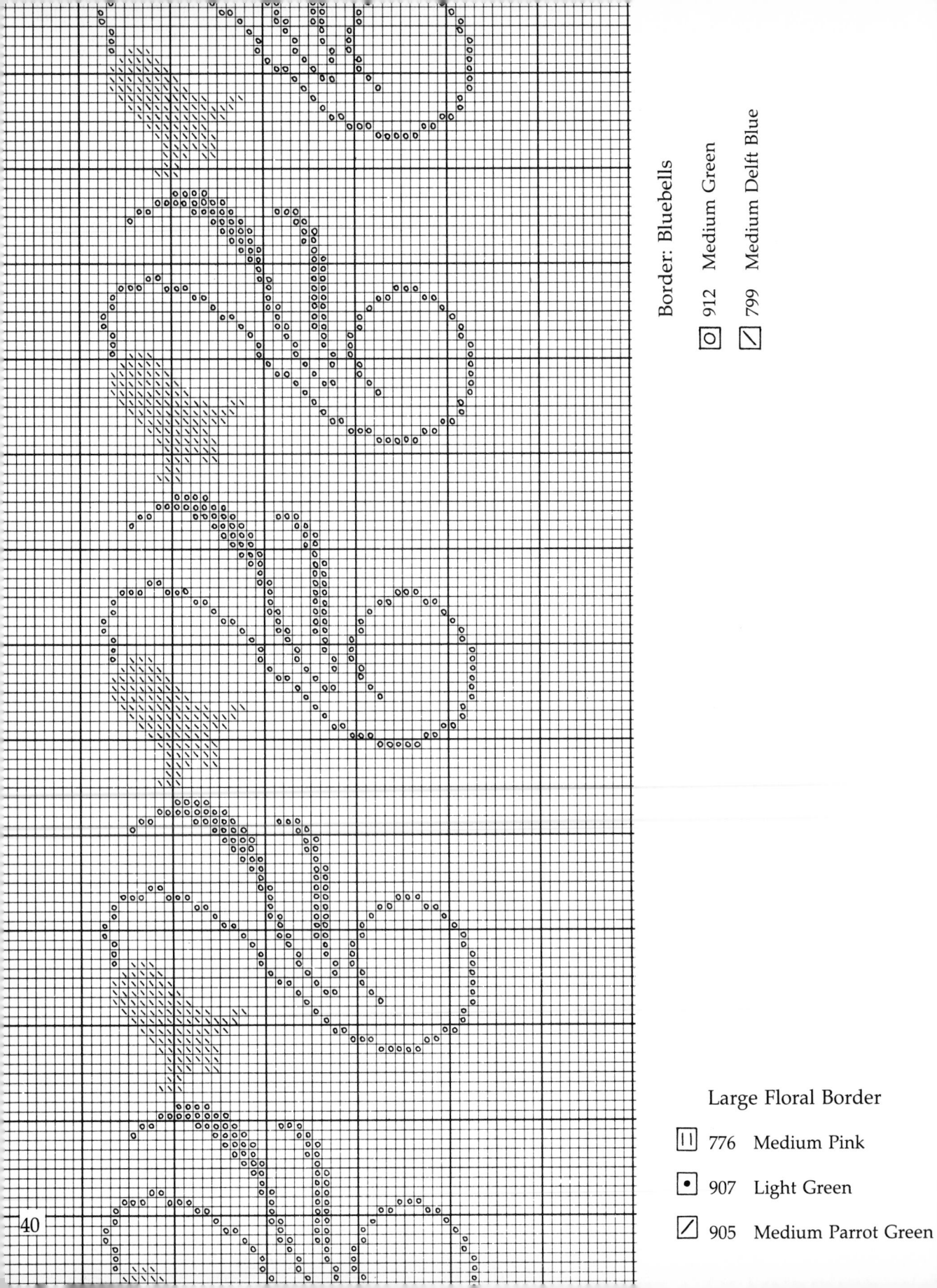

Border: Bluebells

| | 912 | Medium Green |
| | 799 | Medium Delft Blue |

Large Floral Border

	776	Medium Pink
	907	Light Green
	905	Medium Parrot Green

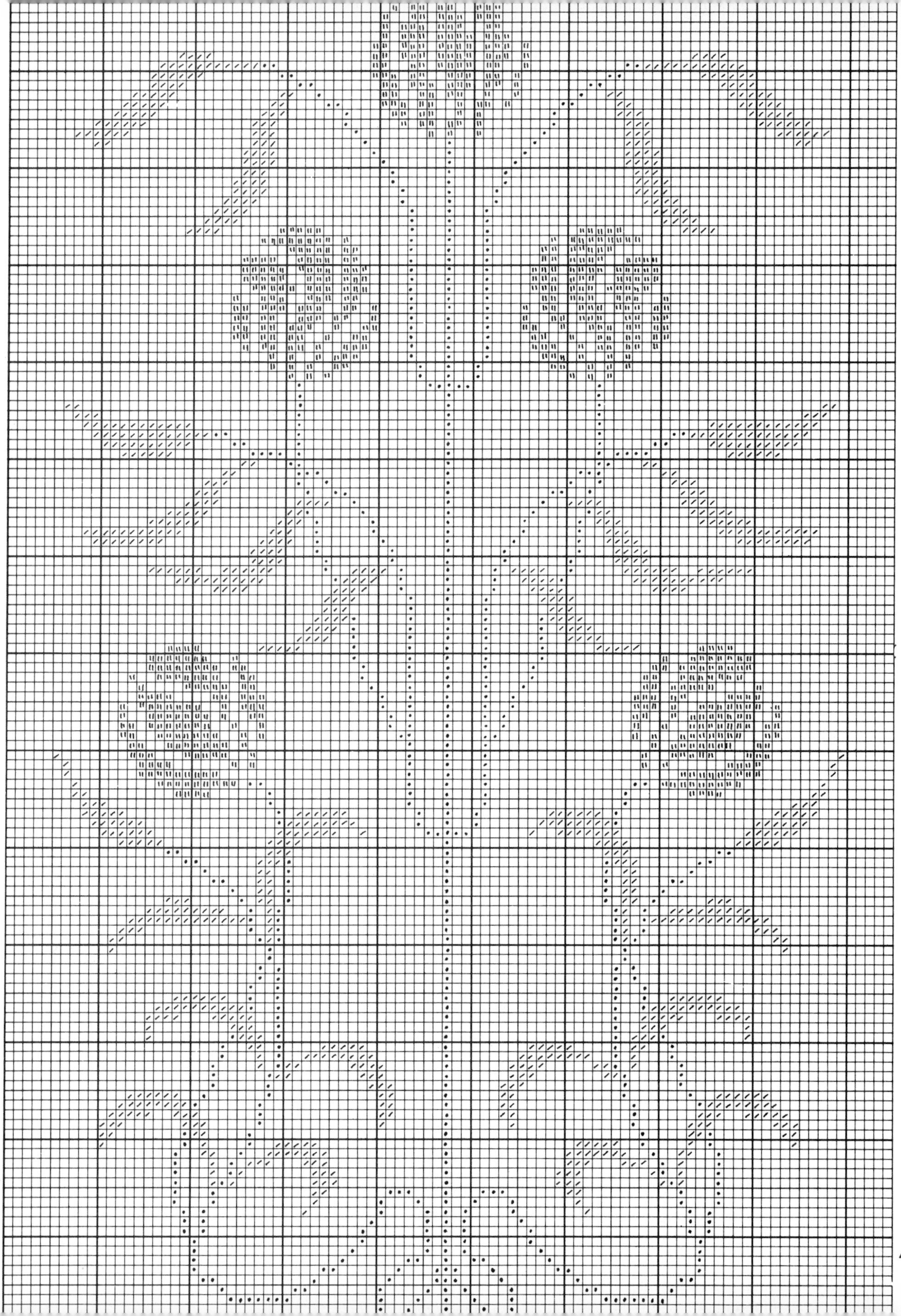

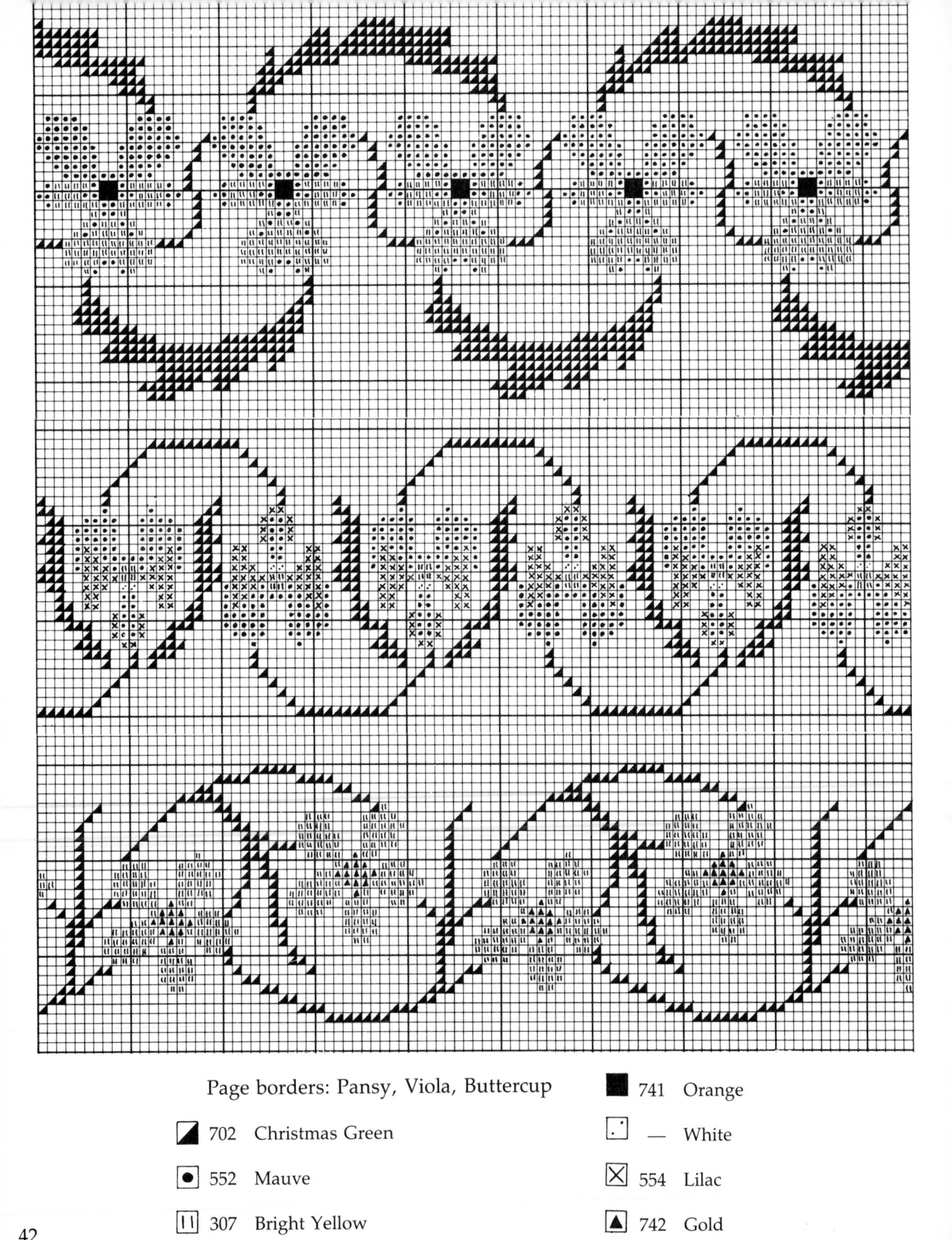

Page borders: Pansy, Viola, Buttercup

◢	702	Christmas Green
●	552	Mauve
II	307	Bright Yellow

■	741	Orange
⊡	—	White
⊠	554	Lilac
▲	742	Gold

42

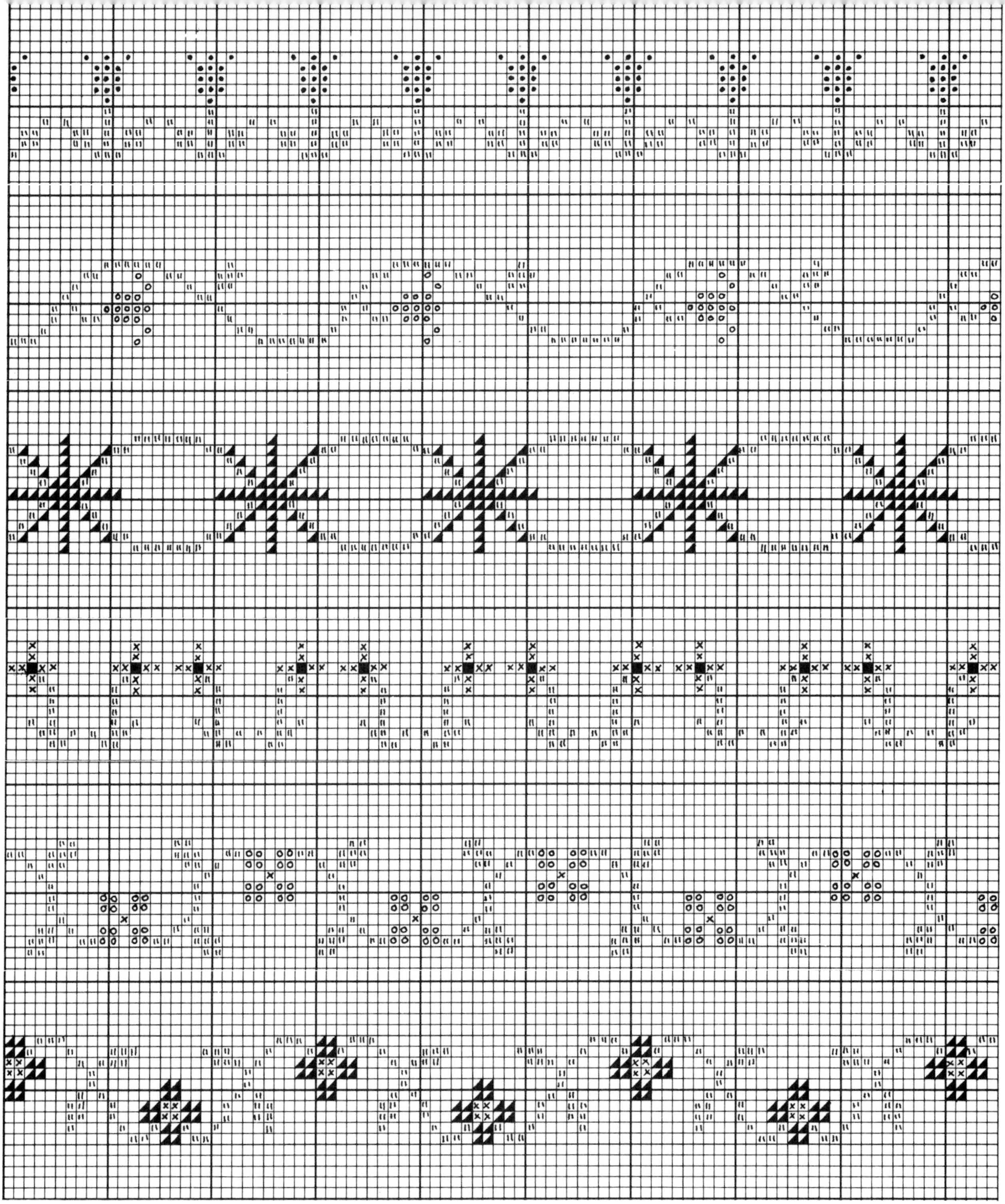

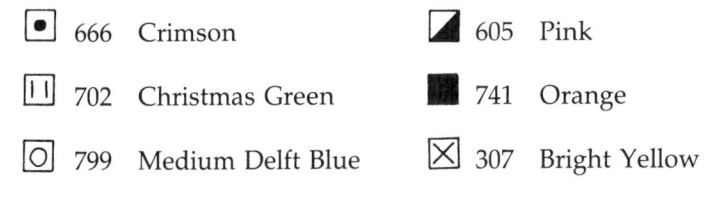

Page borders: Tulip, Bluebell, Ragged Robin, Daffodil, Forget-me-not, Dog Rose

• 666 Crimson		◪ 605 Pink	
⊞ 702 Christmas Green		■ 741 Orange	
⊡ 799 Medium Delft Blue		☒ 307 Bright Yellow	

43

Floral alphabet

Decorative initials are always sought after by
needleworkers, eager to add a distinctive touch to clothes,
samplers, pillows and many other items. Here you will find
a beautiful alphabet embellished with delicate wild flowers.
Each letter illustrates an appropriate flower, and these are
listed in the index.

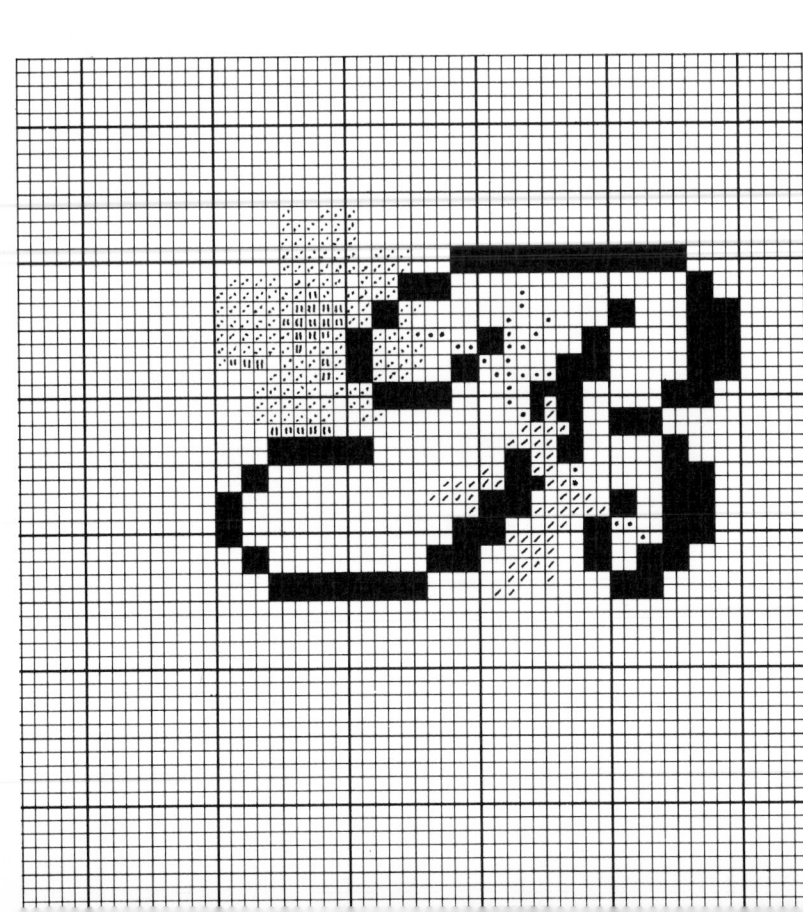

A

■ 796 Dark Royal Blue

⊡ 368 Sage Green

⊡ — White

⊘ 320 Pistachio Green

⊙ 818 Baby Pink

⊞ 3345 Forest Green

⊠ 415 Pale Grey

⊻ 744 Yellow

B

■ 796 Dark Royal Blue

⊡ 703 Chartreuse

⊡ 307 Bright Yellow

⊘ 701 Medium Christmas Green

⊞ 742 Gold

C

	796	Dark Royal Blue
V	744	Yellow
⊡	603	Dark Pink
⊘	954	Light Green
⊞	912	Medium Green
⊡	955	Pale Green

D

	796	Dark Royal Blue
⊡	955	Pale Green
⊘	912	Medium Green
⊞	909	Deep Emerald
⊡	745	Pale Yellow
V	744	Yellow
⊠	743	Deep Yellow
⊙	742	Gold

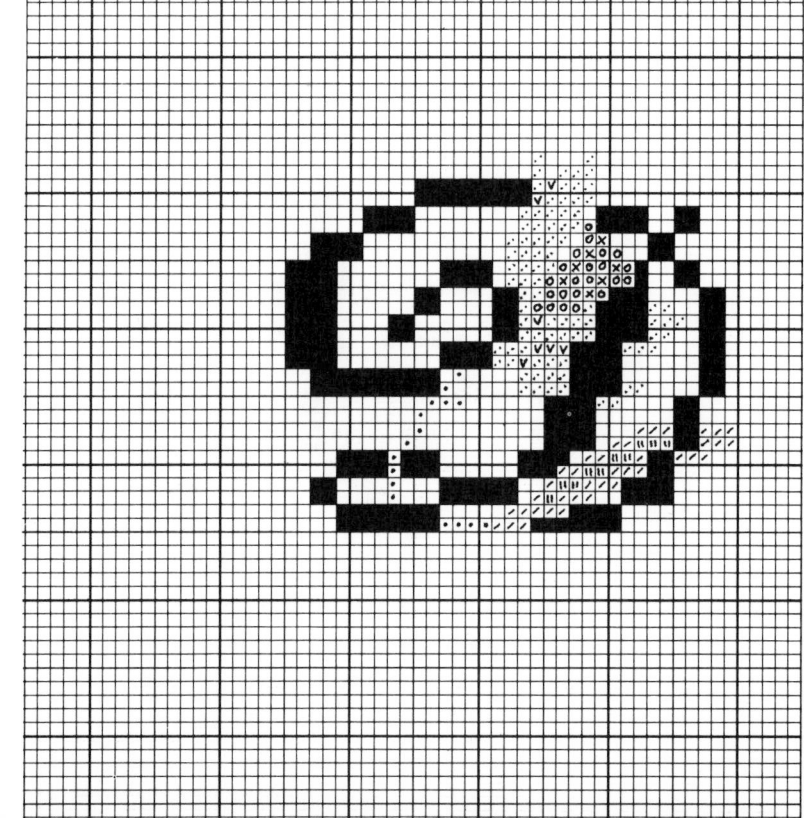

47

E

	796	Dark Royal Blue
⬛	796	Dark Royal Blue
⊡	605	Pink
⊙	703	Chartreuse
V	604	Medium Pink
O	603	Dark Pink
X	335	Deep Rose
II	—	White
N	415	Pale Grey

F

	796	Dark Royal Blue
⬛	796	Dark Royal Blue
⊙	907	Light Green
⊡	818	Baby Pink
╱	906	Parrot Green
II	904	Dark Parrot Green
O	—	White
V	776	Medium Pink

G

- ■ 796 Dark Royal Blue
- · 907 Light Green
- ◢ 905 Medium Parrot Green
- ⊡ 210 Lilac
- Ⓞ 553 Light Mauve
- ☒ — Ecru

H

- ■ 796 Dark Royal Blue
- ⊡ 344 Light Blue
- · 954 Light Green

I

■	796	Dark Royal Blue
•	304	Dark Red
∴	813	Light Blue
V	744	Yellow
X	826	Medium Blue
II	954	Light Green
/	912	Medium Green
O	909	Deep Emerald

J

■	796	Dark Royal Blue
•	906	Parrot Green
II	907	Light Green
∴	744	Yellow
O	444	Buttercup Yellow

K

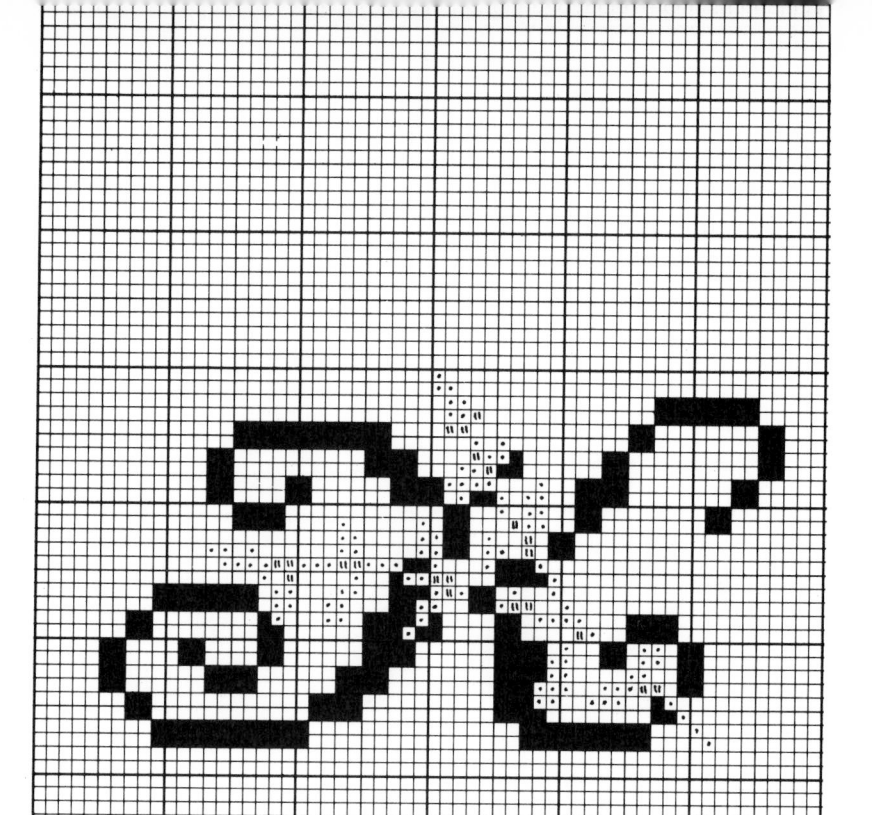

- ■ 796   Dark Royal Blue
- ⊡ 906   Parrot Green
- ⊞ 335   Deep Rose

L

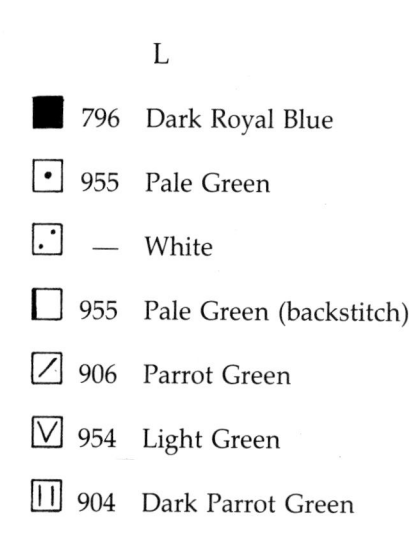

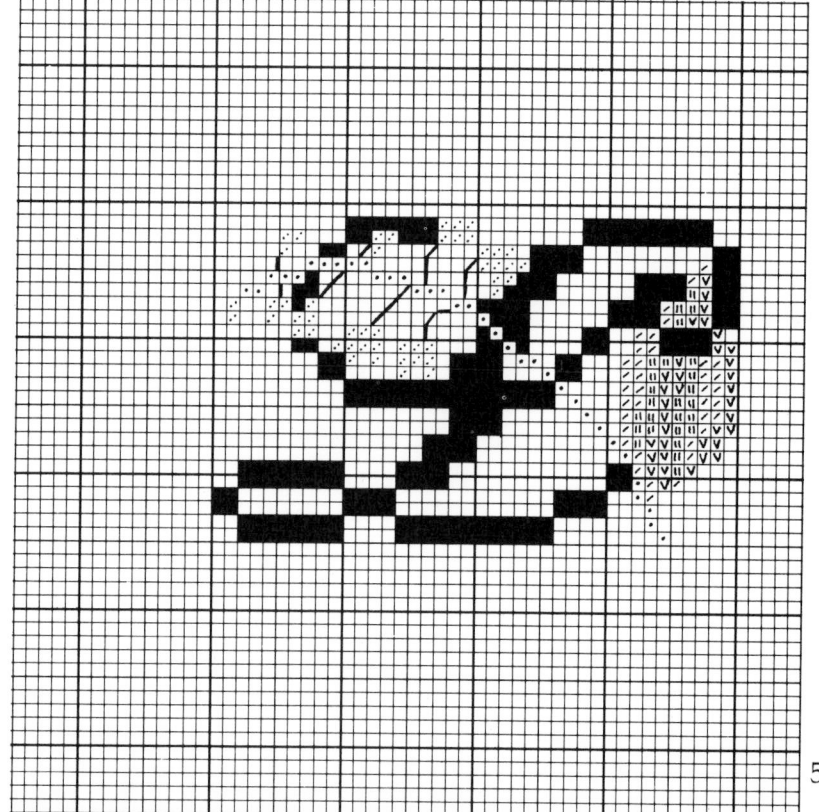

- ■ 796   Dark Royal Blue
- ⊡ 955   Pale Green
- ⊡ —   White
- ☐ 955   Pale Green (backstitch)
- ⧄ 906   Parrot Green
- ⩔ 954   Light Green
- ⊞ 904   Dark Parrot Green

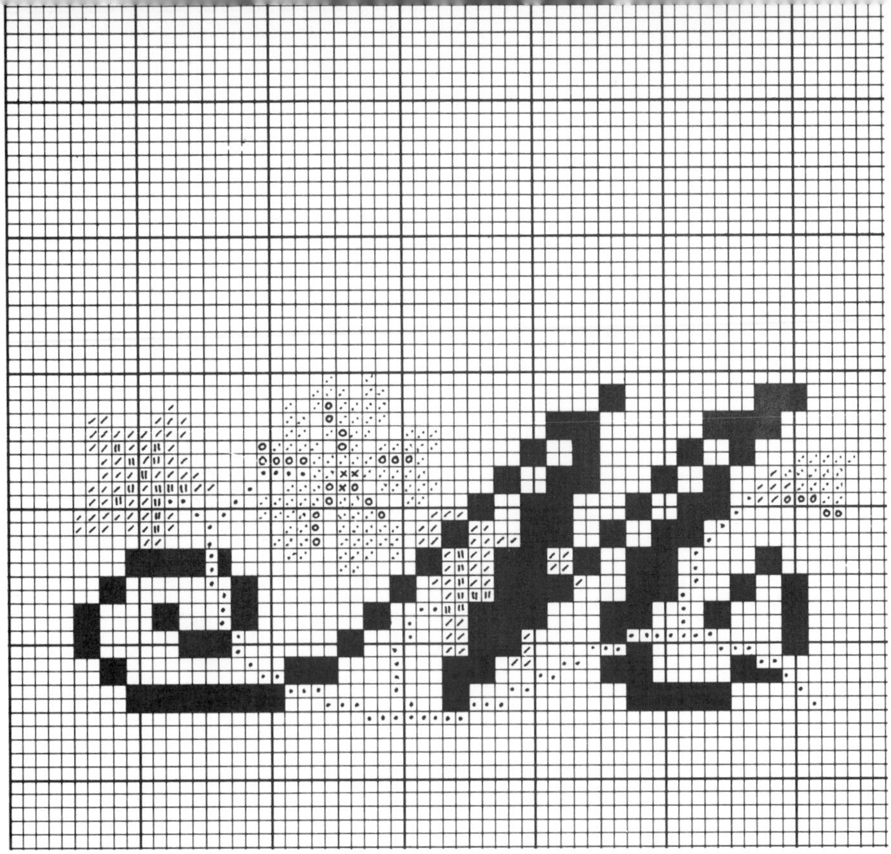

M

796 Dark Royal Blue

320 Pistachio Green

906 Parrot Green

904 Dark Parrot Green

3688 Light Mulberry

3686 Dark Mulberry

— White

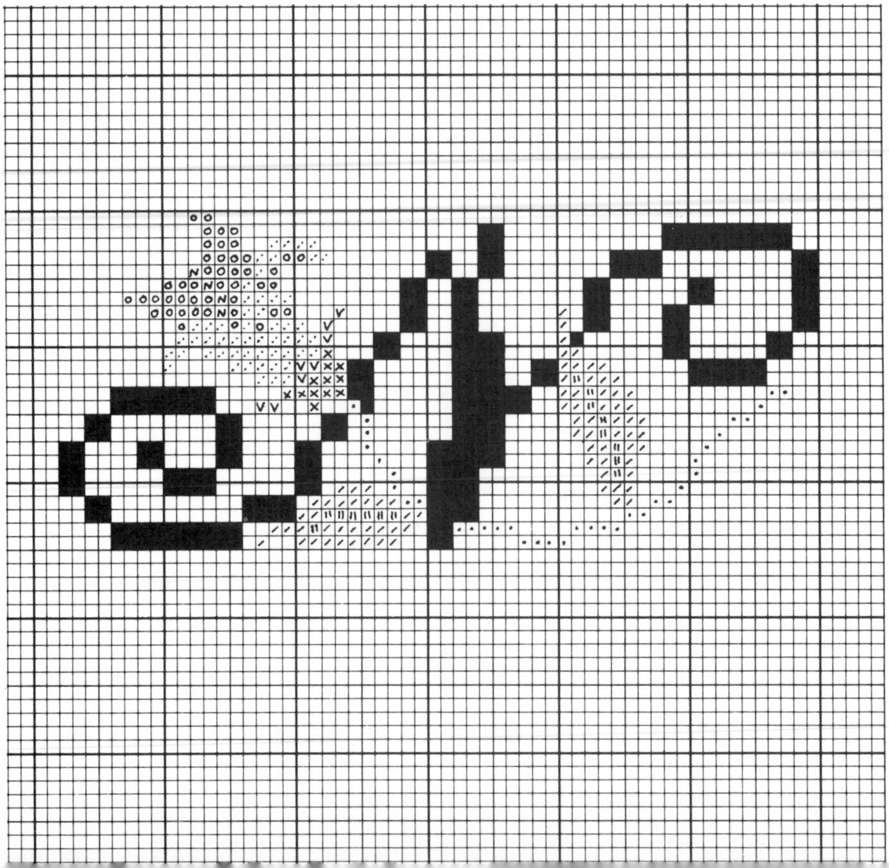

N

796 Dark Royal Blue

906 Parrot Green

907 Light Green

905 Medium Parrot Green

210 Lilac

703 Chartreuse

436 Tan

553 Light Mauve

— Ecru

O

■	796	Dark Royal Blue
⊡	906	Parrot Green
⧄	904	Dark Parrot Green
Ⅴ	415	Pale Grey
Ⓞ	743	Deep Yellow
⊡	—	White

P

■	796	Dark Royal Blue
⊡	907	Light Green
⧄	700	Medium Christmas Green
⊡	900	Very Deep Orange
Ⅴ	304	Red
Ⓞ	318	Medium Grey
⊠	310	Black

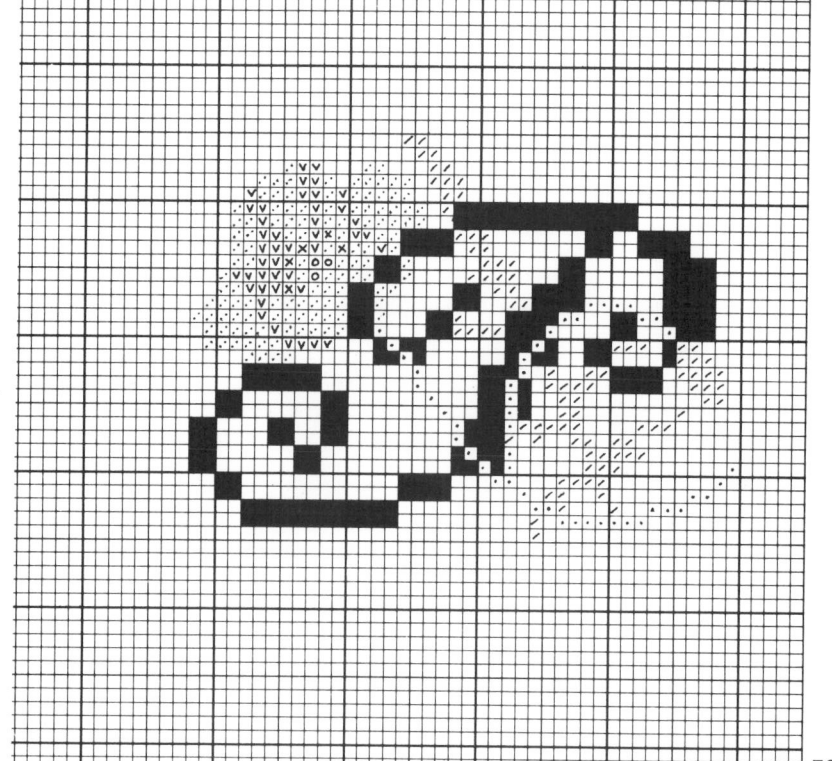

53

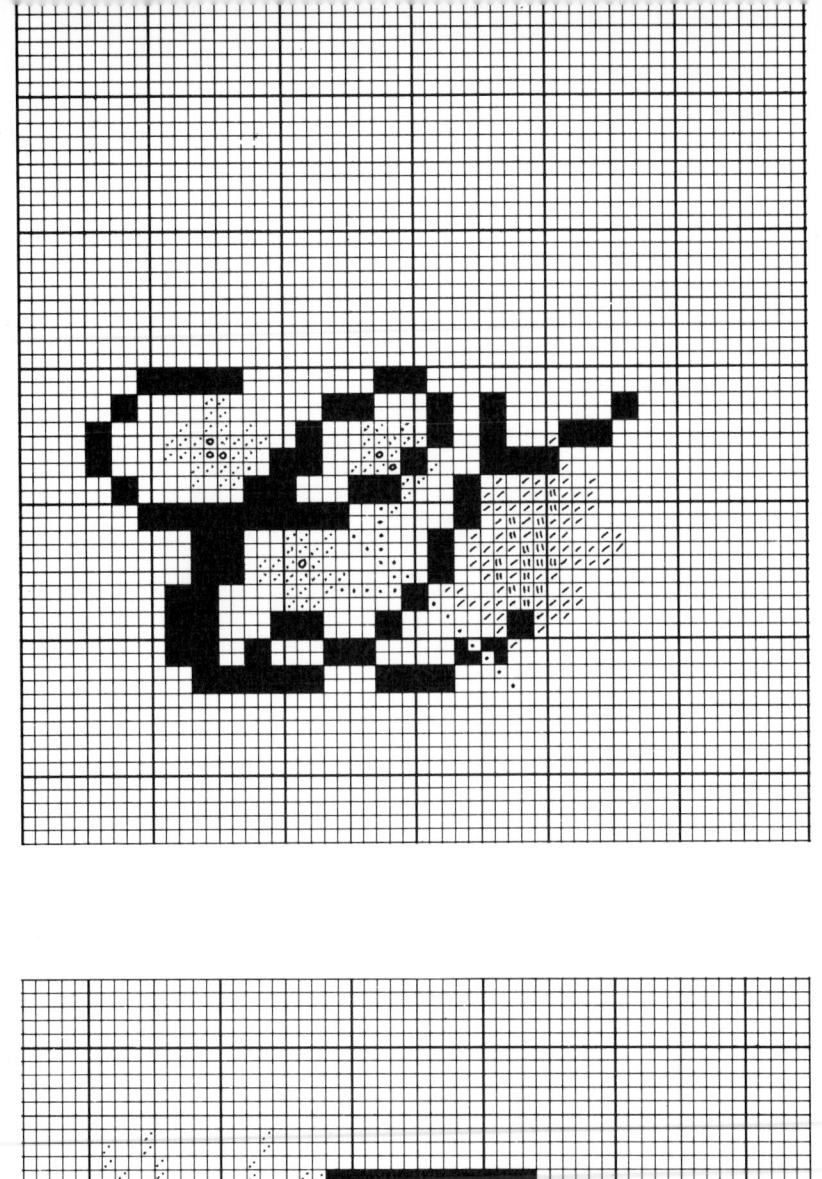

Q

■	796	Dark Royal Blue
⟋	906	Parrot Green
‖	745	Pale Yellow
•	907	Light Green
∴	818	Baby Pink
Ⓞ	742	Gold

R

■	796	Dark Royal Blue
⟋	906	Parrot Green
•	907	Light Green
∴	3326	Rose Pink

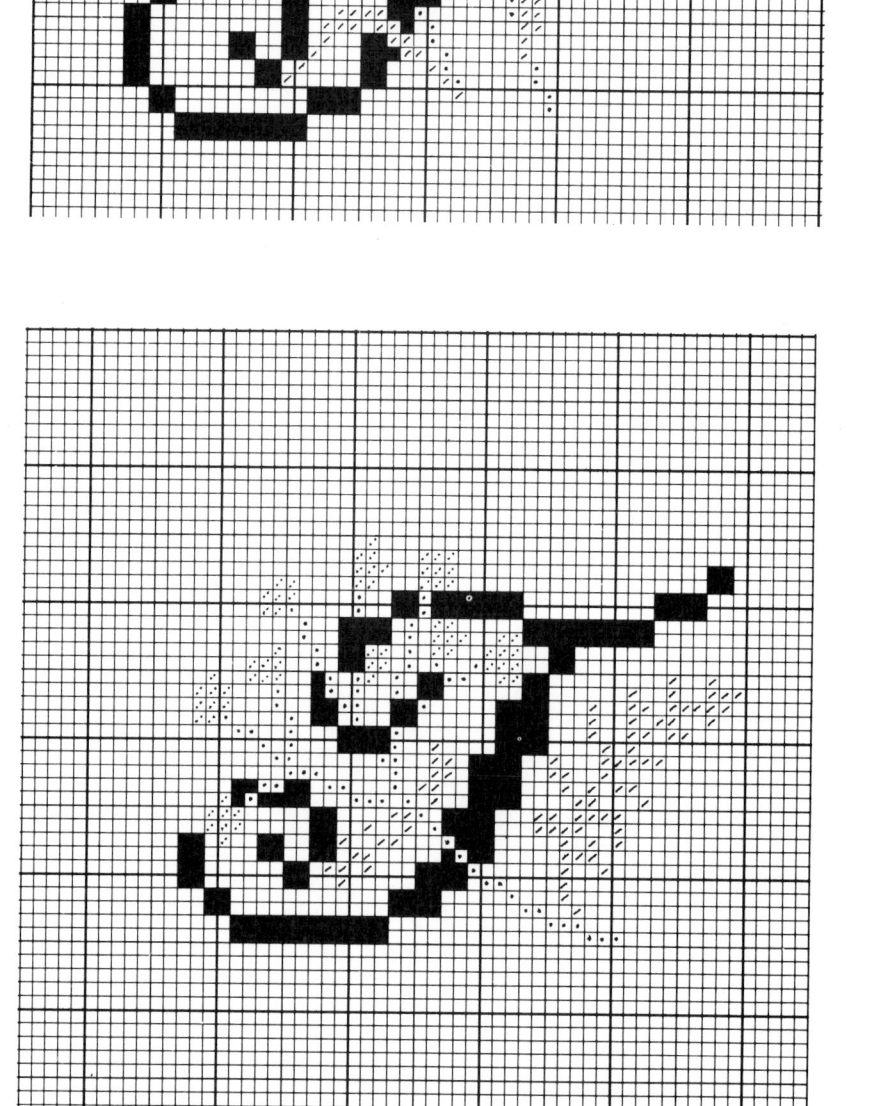

S

	796	Dark Royal Blue
◪	954	Light Green
⊡	955	Pale Green
⊙	415	Pale Grey
▽	952	Medium-Light Green
⊡	—	White

T

	796	Dark Royal Blue
⊡	368	Sage Green
⊡	743	Deep Yellow
◪	820	Pistachio Green

55

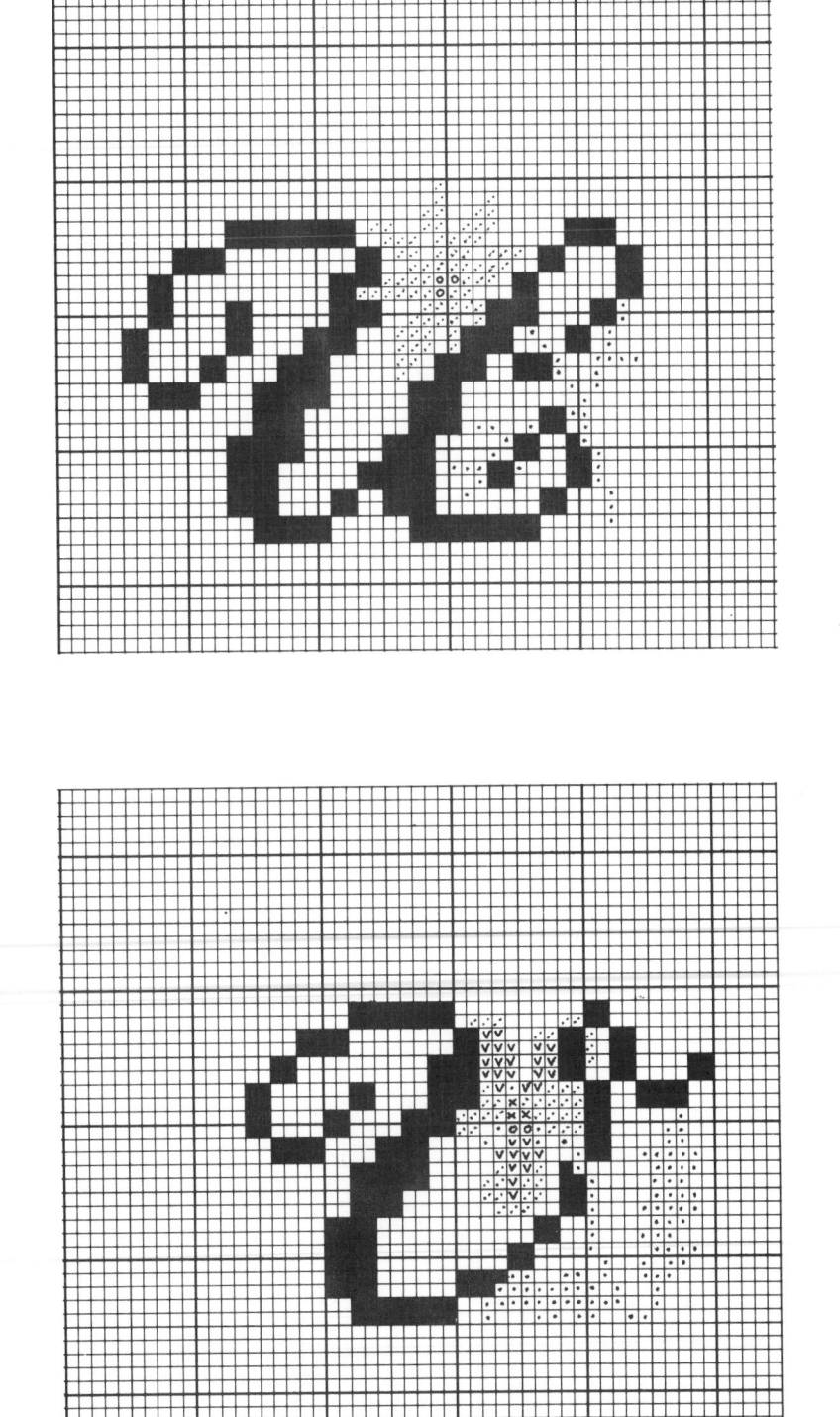

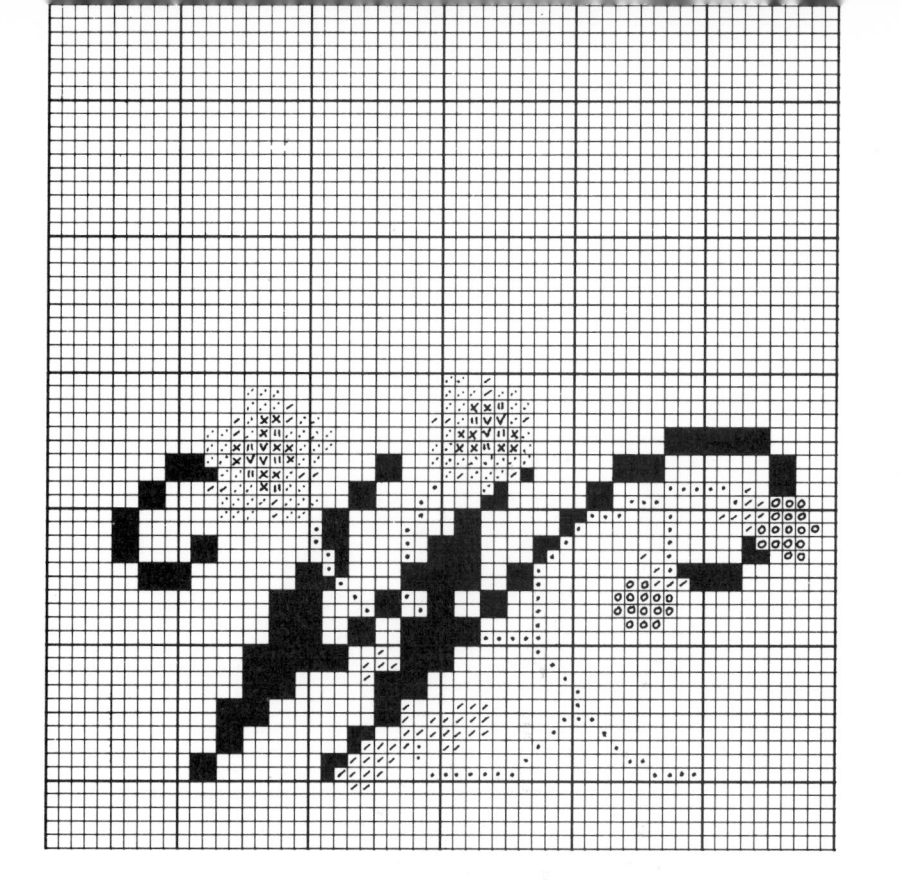

W

■	796	Dark Royal Blue
⊡	954	Light Green
⊘	906	Parrot Green
⊙	351	Pale Orange-Red
⊡	—	White
⊠	415	Pale Grey
⊞	744	Yellow
⊻	955	Pale Green

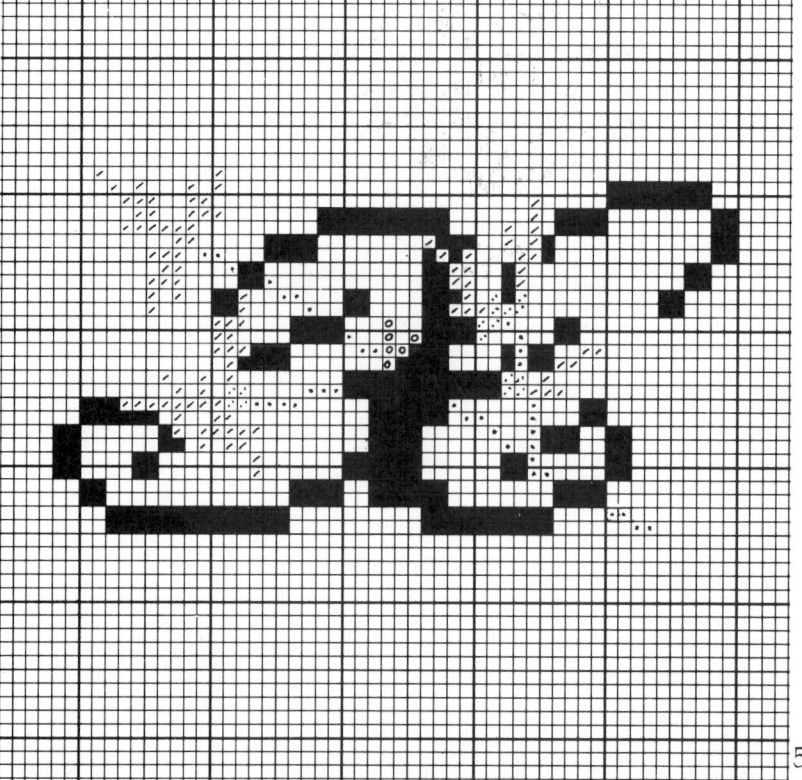

X

■	796	Dark Royal Blue
⊡	955	Pale Green
⊙	738	Very Light Tan
⊘	911	Emerald
⊡	—	Ecru

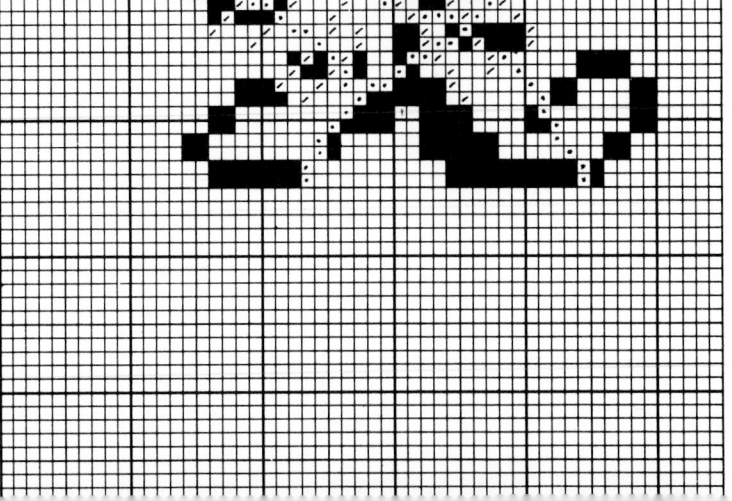

Y

■ 796 Dark Royal Blue

• 955 Pale Green

⁄ 954 Light Green

‖ 912 Medium Green

∴ 744 Yellow

Z

■ 796 Dark Royal Blue

• 907 Light Green

⁄ 904 Dark Parrot Green

∴ 335 Deep Rose

Wild flowers in their natural form

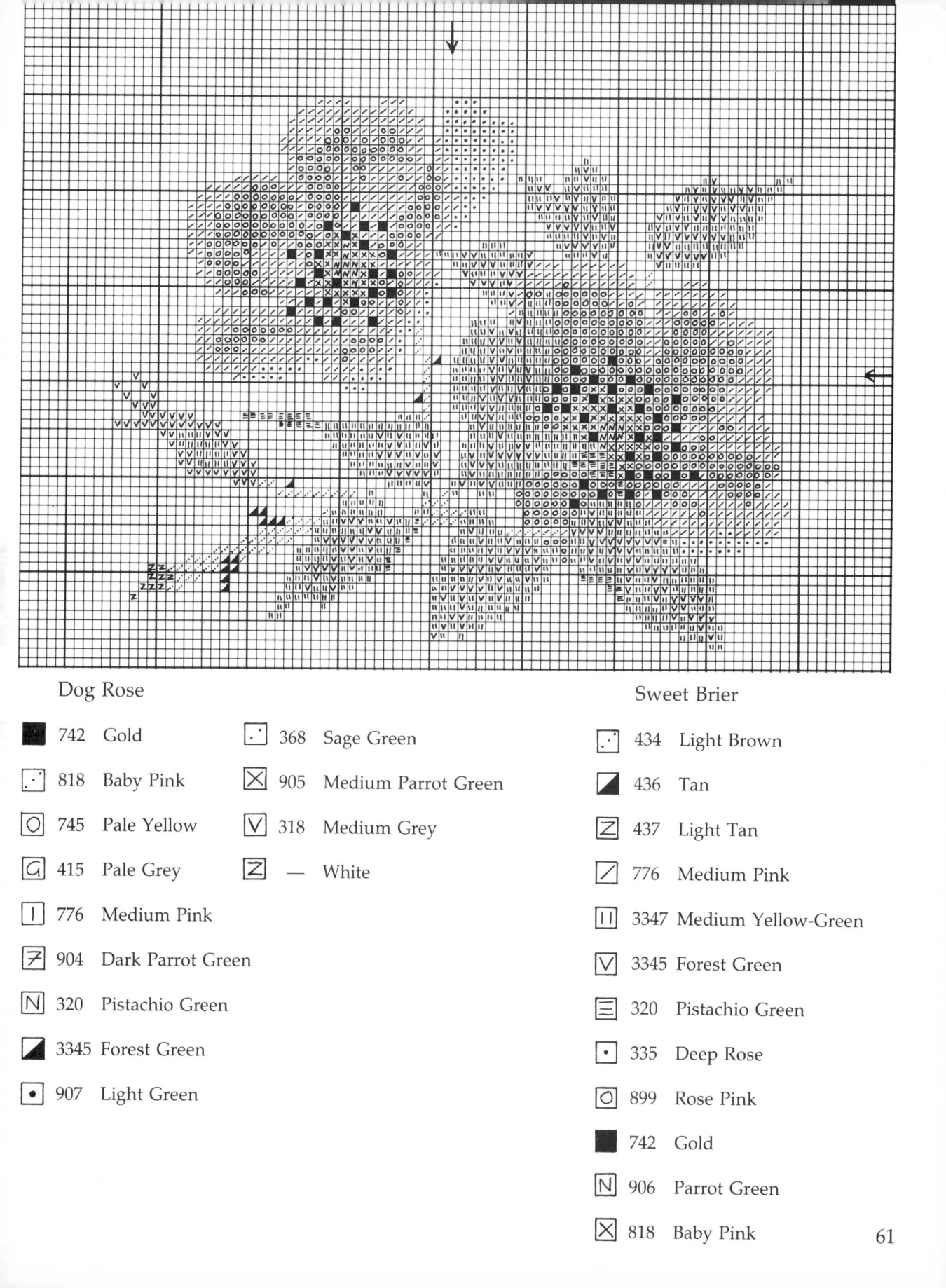

Dog Rose

■	742	Gold	⊡	368	Sage Green
⊡	818	Baby Pink	⊠	905	Medium Parrot Green
⊙	745	Pale Yellow	⊻	318	Medium Grey
⊡	415	Pale Grey	⊵	—	White
⊡	776	Medium Pink			
⊅	904	Dark Parrot Green			
⊠	320	Pistachio Green			
◪	3345	Forest Green			
⊡	907	Light Green			

Sweet Brier

⊡	434	Light Brown
◪	436	Tan
⊡	437	Light Tan
⊡	776	Medium Pink
⊡	3347	Medium Yellow-Green
⊻	3345	Forest Green
☰	320	Pistachio Green
•	335	Deep Rose
⊙	899	Rose Pink
■	742	Gold
⊠	906	Parrot Green
⊠	818	Baby Pink

Daffodil

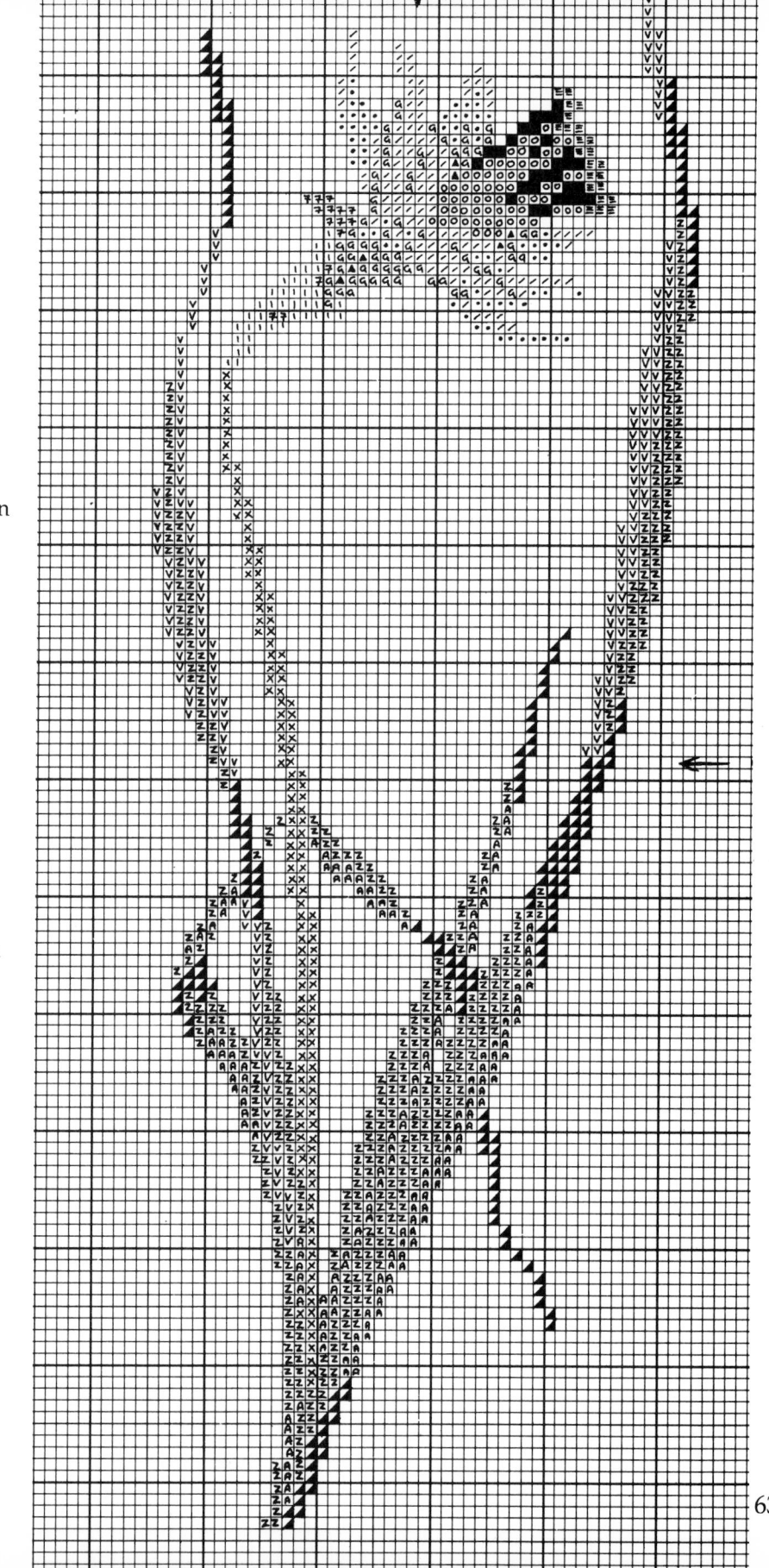	699	Dark Christmas Green
Z	955	Pale Green
A	912	Medium Green
/	745	Pale Yellow
·	307	Bright Yellow
G	415	Pale Grey
X	368	Sage Green
∴	954	Light Green
V	905	Medium Parrot Green
▲	445	Lemon Yellow
■	741	Orange
O	444	Buttercup Yellow
II	744	Yellow
☰	743	Deep Yellow
Ƶ	919	Dark Copper
I	318	Medium Grey
6	644	Fawn
∵	320	Pistachio Green
⊠	742	Gold

63

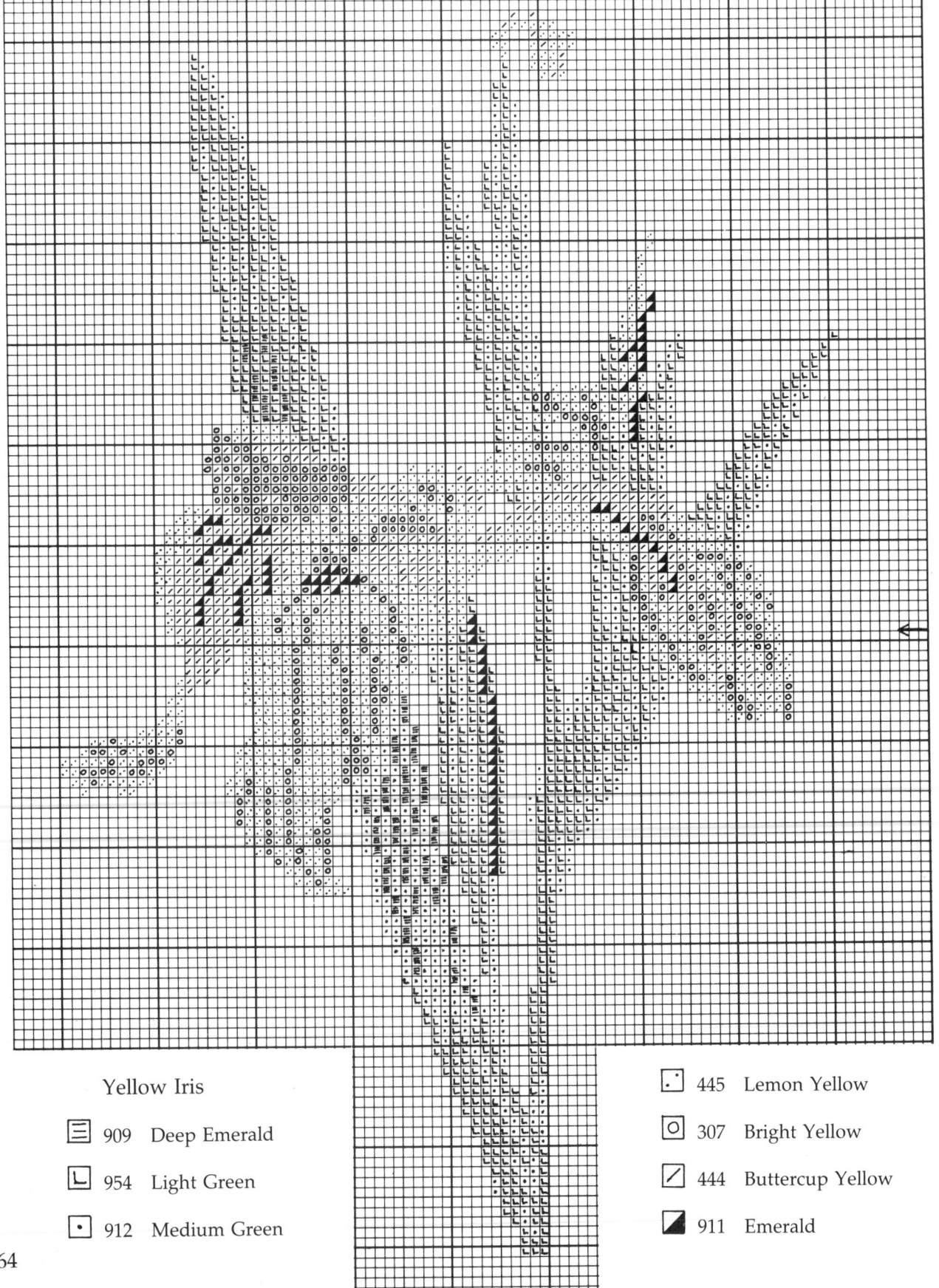

Yellow Iris

	909	Deep Emerald
	954	Light Green
	912	Medium Green

	445	Lemon Yellow
	307	Bright Yellow
	444	Buttercup Yellow
	911	Emerald

Meadow Cranesbill

■	796	Dark Royal Blue	⊠	368	Sage Green
N	798	Dark Delft Blue	Z	841	Beige-Brown
O	799	Medium Delft Blue	‖	909	Deep Emerald
◢	—	Ecru	□	895	Dark Forest Green (backstitch)
⅂	644	Fawn	⊟	700	Medium Christmas Green
⣀	3325	Baby Blue	╱	702	Christmas Green

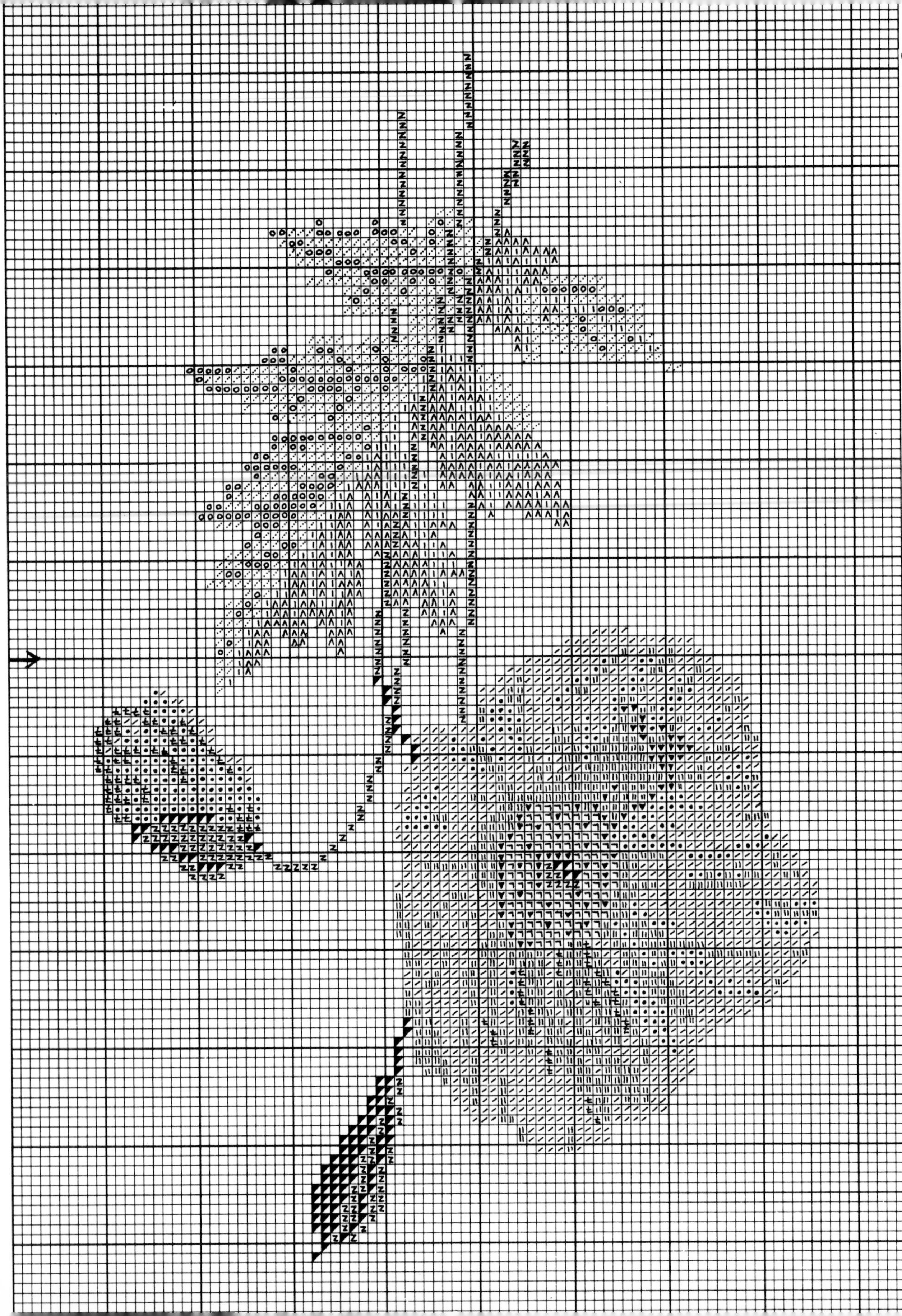

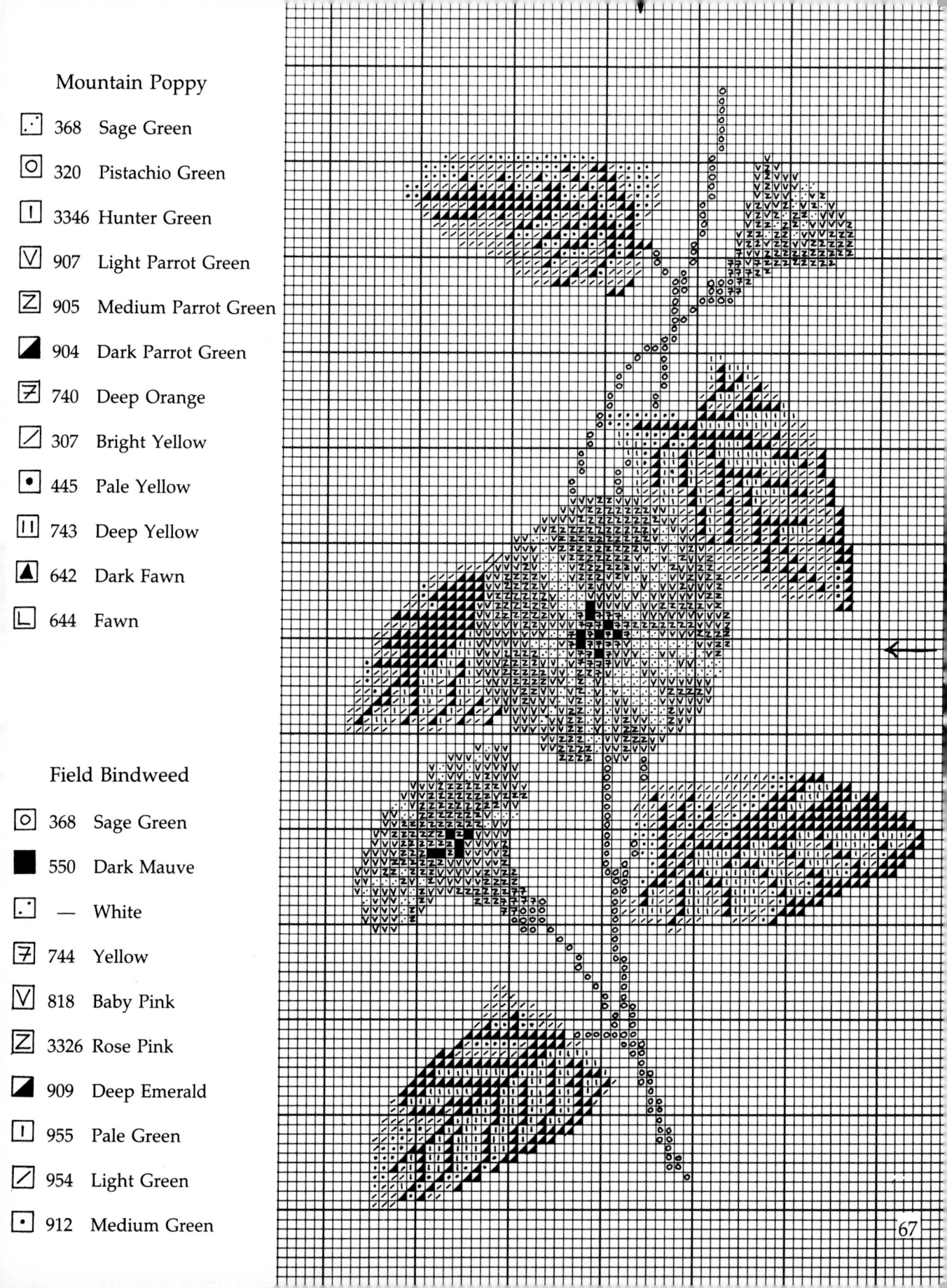

Mountain Poppy

⌁	368	Sage Green
O	320	Pistachio Green
I	3346	Hunter Green
V	907	Light Parrot Green
Z	905	Medium Parrot Green
◥	904	Dark Parrot Green
⅂	740	Deep Orange
╱	307	Bright Yellow
•	445	Pale Yellow
‖	743	Deep Yellow
▲	642	Dark Fawn
⌐	644	Fawn

Field Bindweed

O	368	Sage Green
■	550	Dark Mauve
⌁	—	White
⅂	744	Yellow
V	818	Baby Pink
Z	3326	Rose Pink
◥	909	Deep Emerald
I	955	Pale Green
╱	954	Light Green
•	912	Medium Green

67

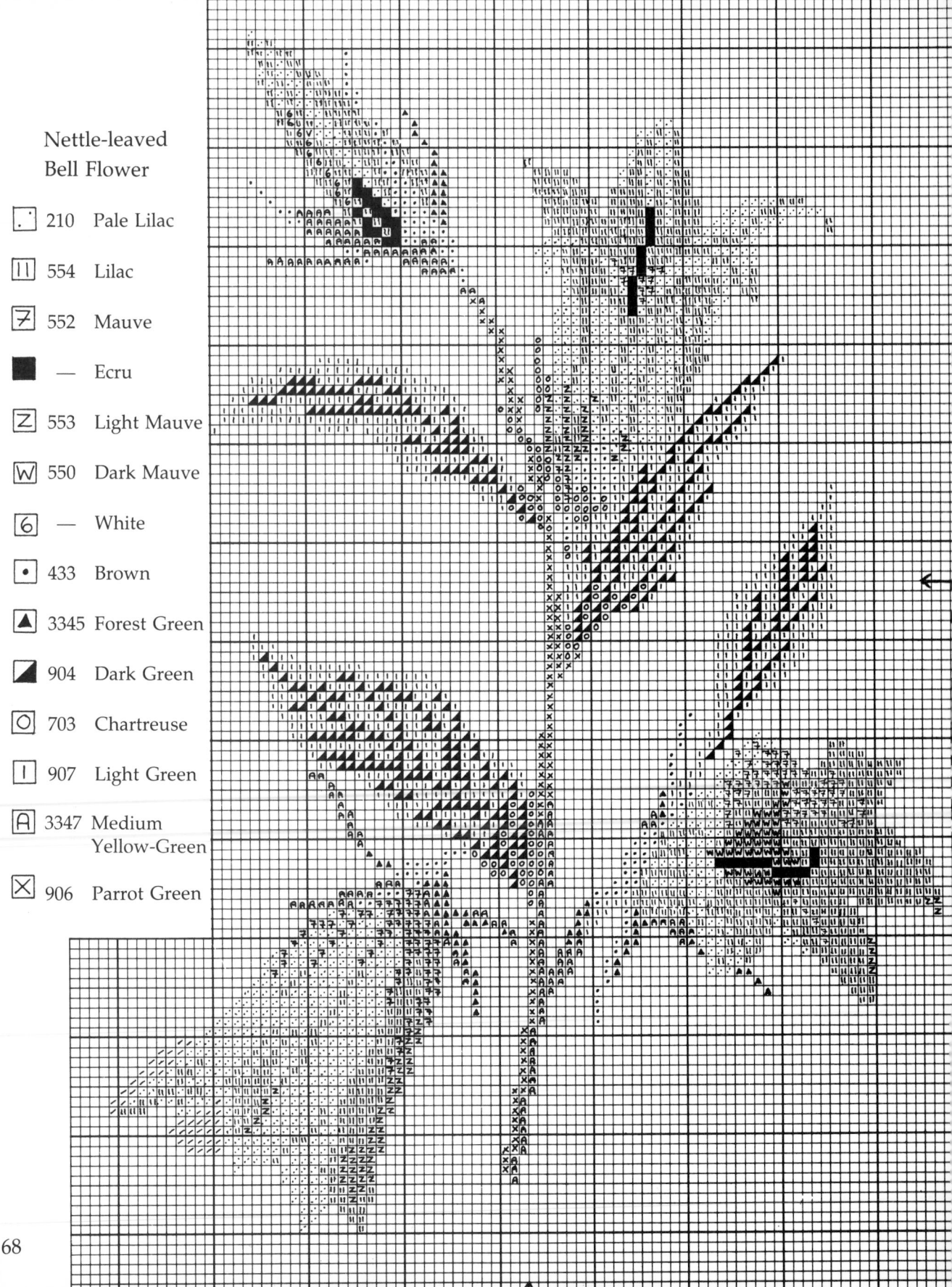

Nettle-leaved
Bell Flower

	210	Pale Lilac
	554	Lilac
	552	Mauve
	—	Ecru
	553	Light Mauve
	550	Dark Mauve
	—	White
	433	Brown
	3345	Forest Green
	904	Dark Green
	703	Chartreuse
	907	Light Green
	3347	Medium Yellow-Green
	906	Parrot Green

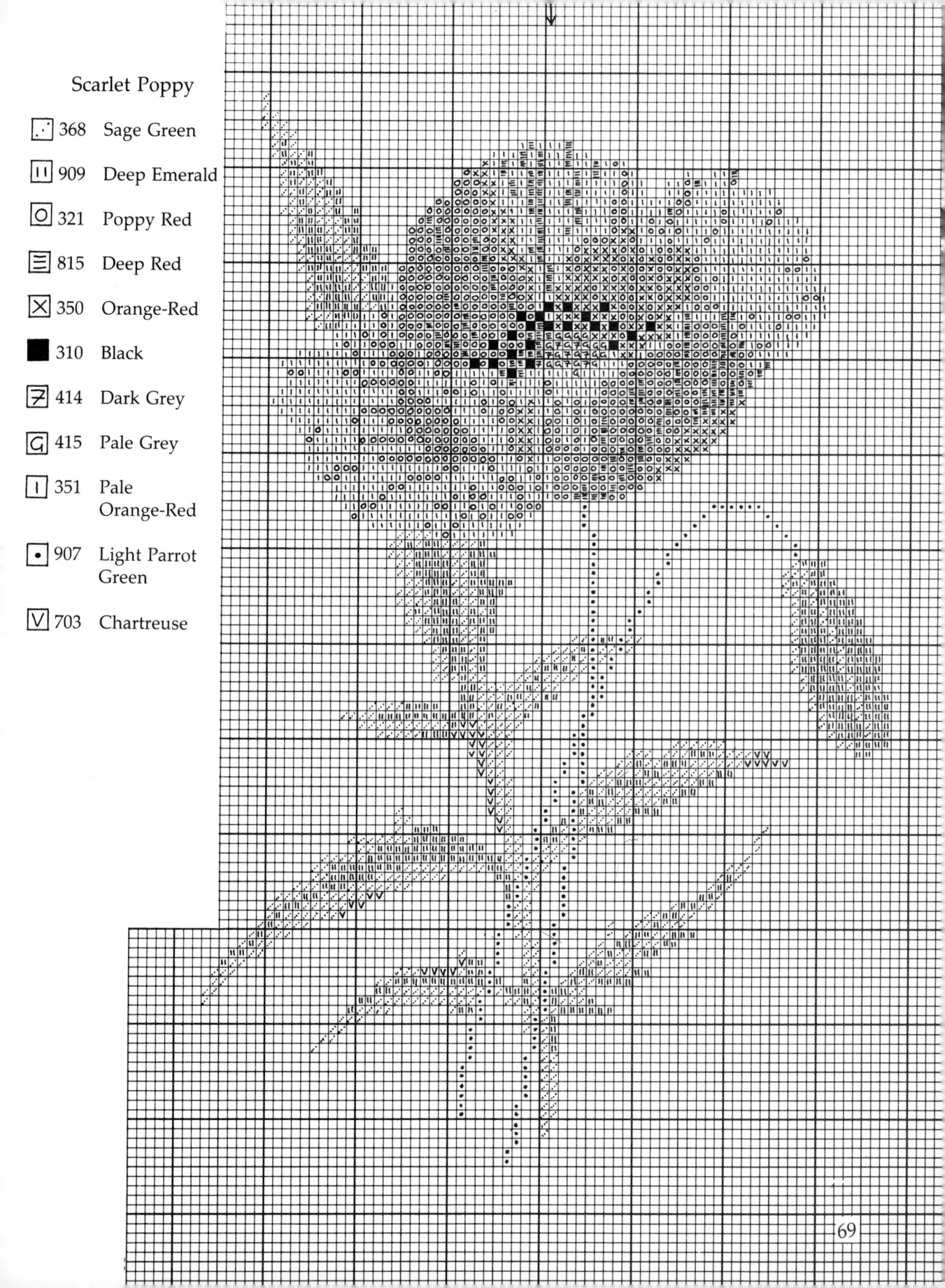

Scarlet Poppy

$\boxed{\because}$	368	Sage Green
$\boxed{II}$	909	Deep Emerald
$\boxed{O}$	321	Poppy Red
$\boxed{\equiv}$	815	Deep Red
$\boxed{X}$	350	Orange-Red
$\boxed{\blacksquare}$	310	Black
$\boxed{7}$	414	Dark Grey
$\boxed{G}$	415	Pale Grey
$\boxed{I}$	351	Pale Orange-Red
$\boxed{\bullet}$	907	Light Parrot Green
$\boxed{V}$	703	Chartreuse

69

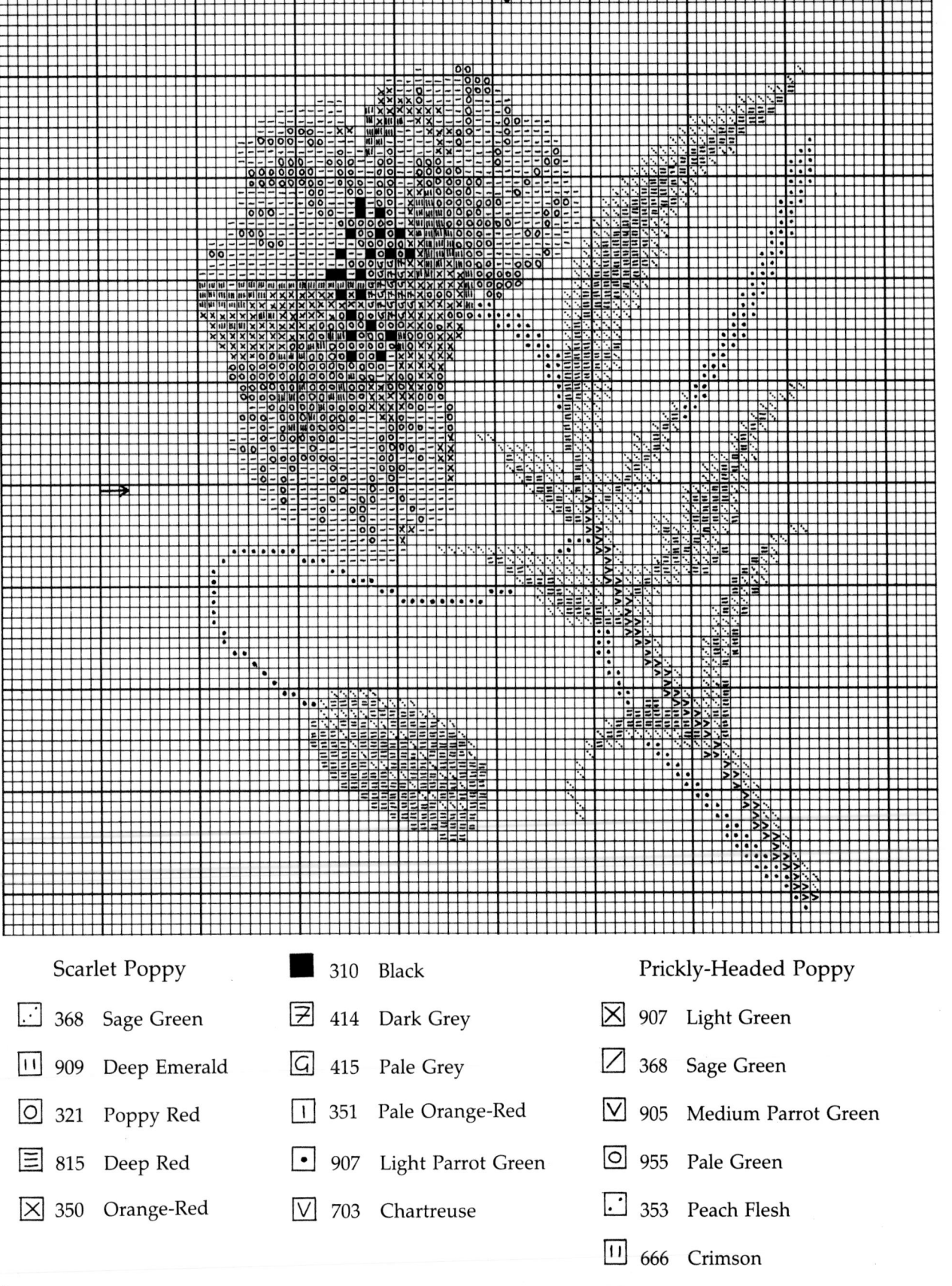

Scarlet Poppy

	368	Sage Green
	909	Deep Emerald
	321	Poppy Red
	815	Deep Red
	350	Orange-Red

	310	Black
	414	Dark Grey
	415	Pale Grey
	351	Pale Orange-Red
	907	Light Parrot Green
	703	Chartreuse

Prickly-Headed Poppy

	907	Light Green
	368	Sage Green
	905	Medium Parrot Green
	955	Pale Green
	353	Peach Flesh
	666	Crimson
	310	Black (backstitch)

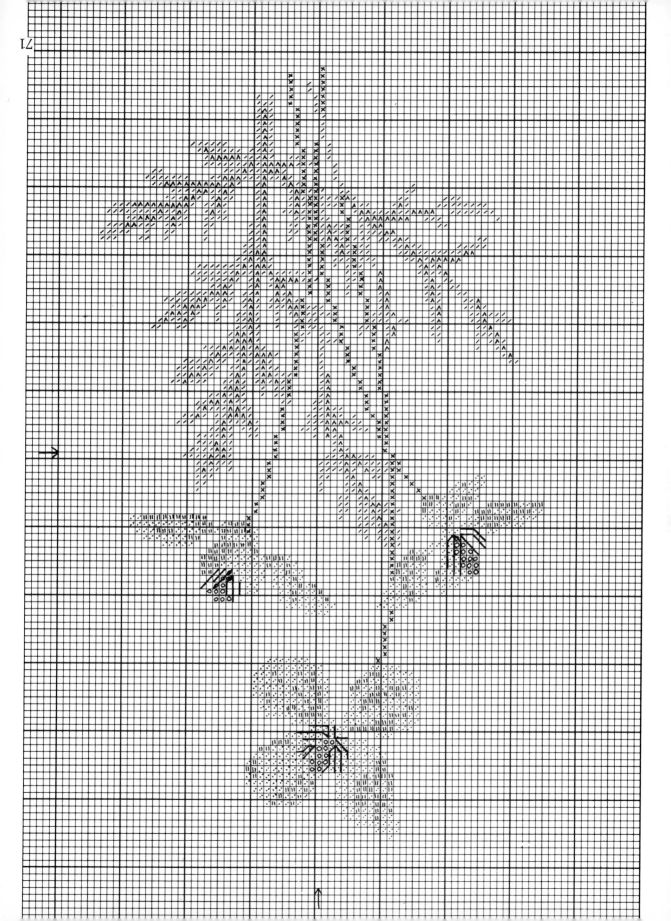

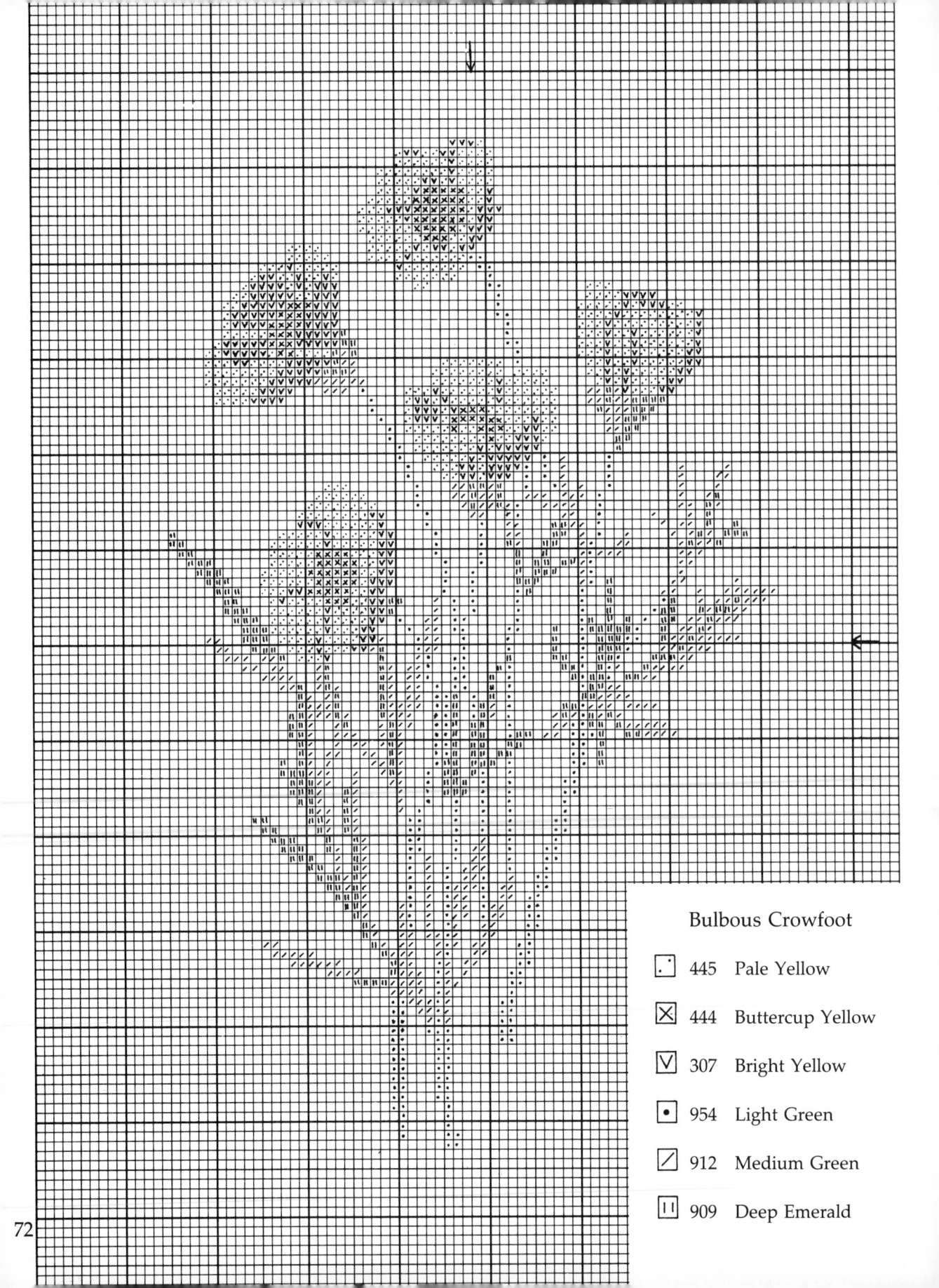

Bulbous Crowfoot

Symbol	Code	Colour
.	445	Pale Yellow
X	444	Buttercup Yellow
V	307	Bright Yellow
•	954	Light Green
/	912	Medium Green
II	909	Deep Emerald

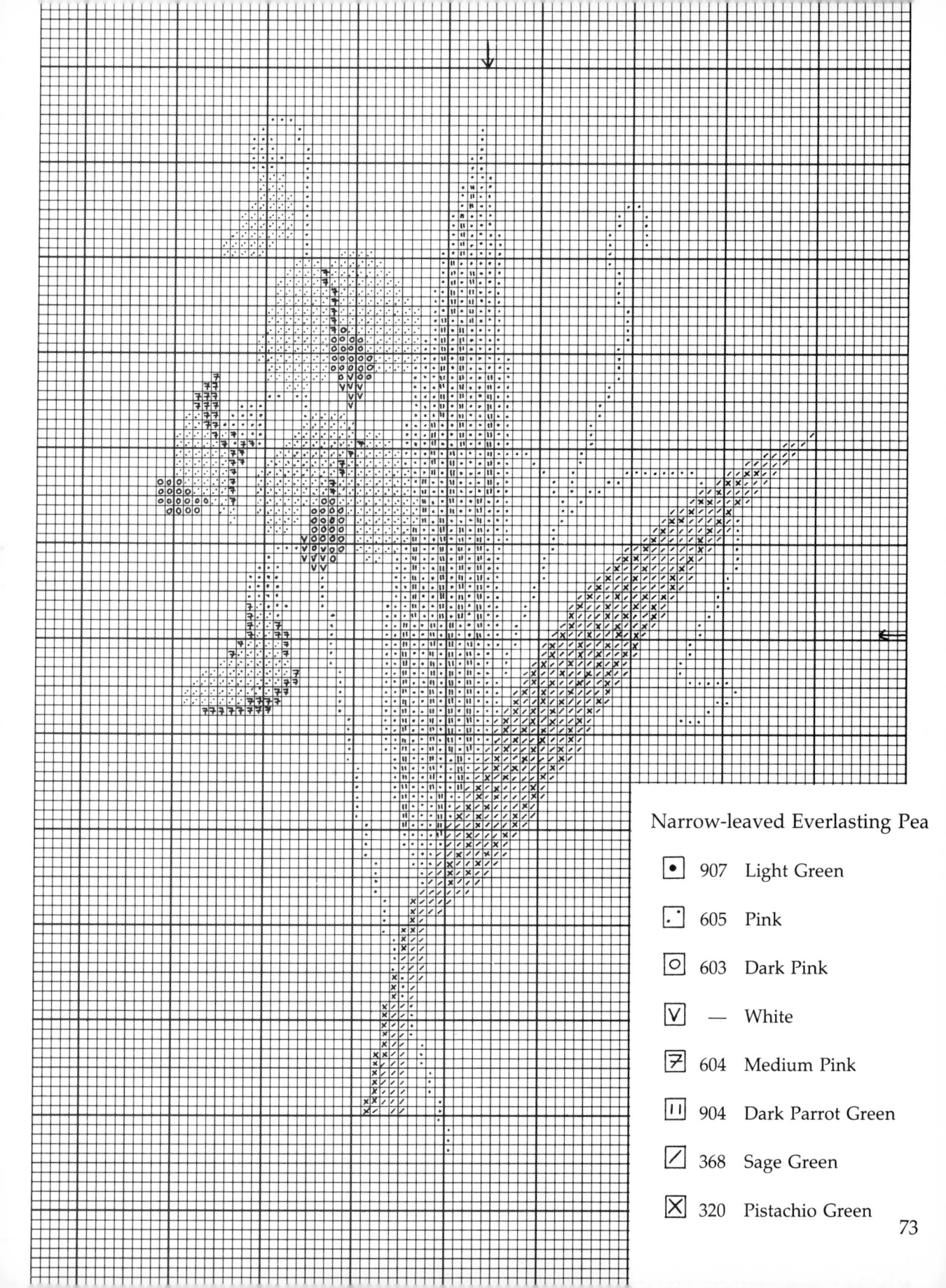

Narrow-leaved Everlasting Pea

•	907	Light Green
.·	605	Pink
O	603	Dark Pink
V	—	White
⇁	604	Medium Pink
‖	904	Dark Parrot Green
╱	368	Sage Green
✕	320	Pistachio Green

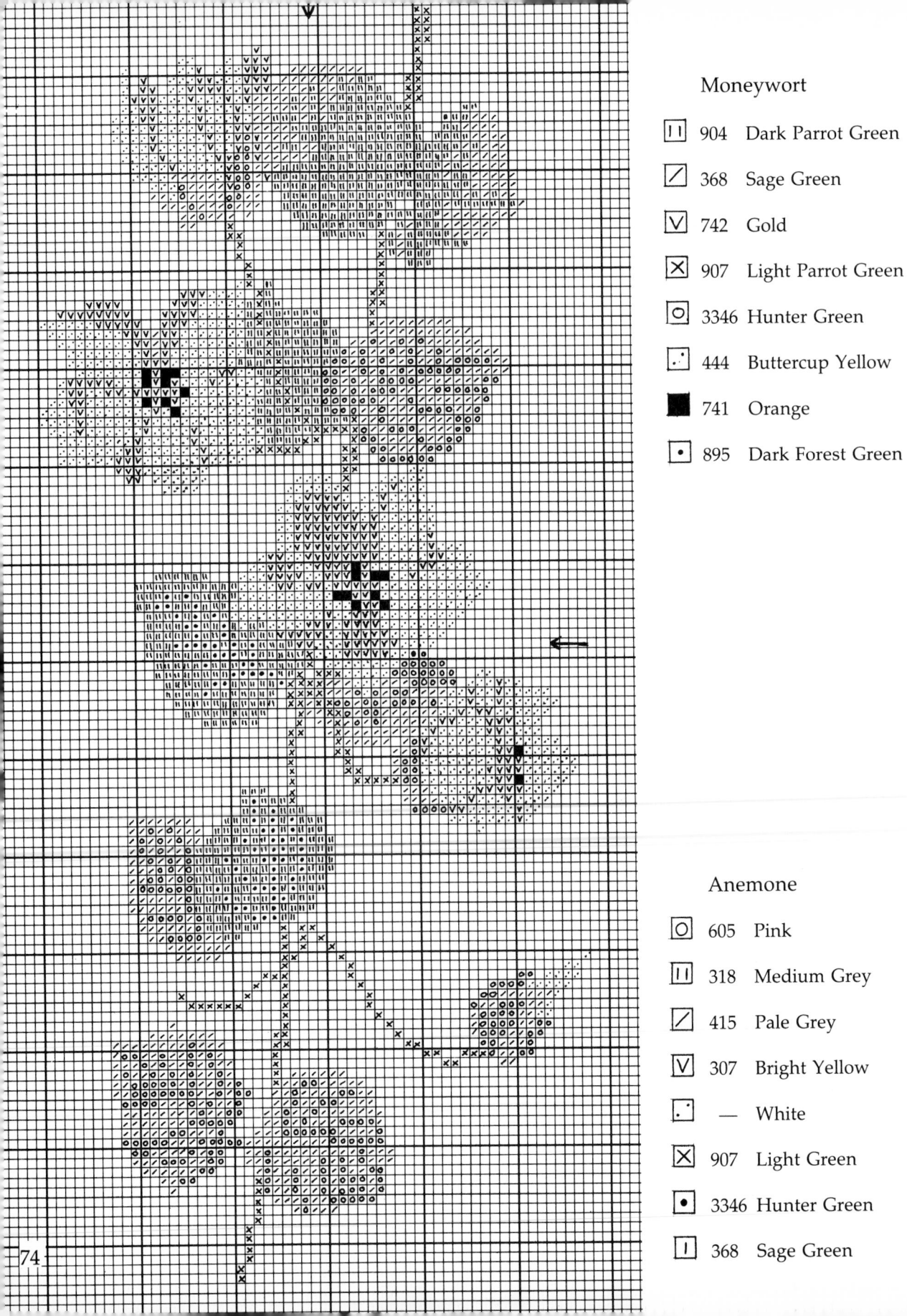

Moneywort

II	904	Dark Parrot Green
/	368	Sage Green
V	742	Gold
X	907	Light Parrot Green
O	3346	Hunter Green
.	444	Buttercup Yellow
■	741	Orange
.	895	Dark Forest Green

Anemone

O	605	Pink
II	318	Medium Grey
/	415	Pale Grey
V	307	Bright Yellow
.	—	White
X	907	Light Green
.	3346	Hunter Green
I	368	Sage Green

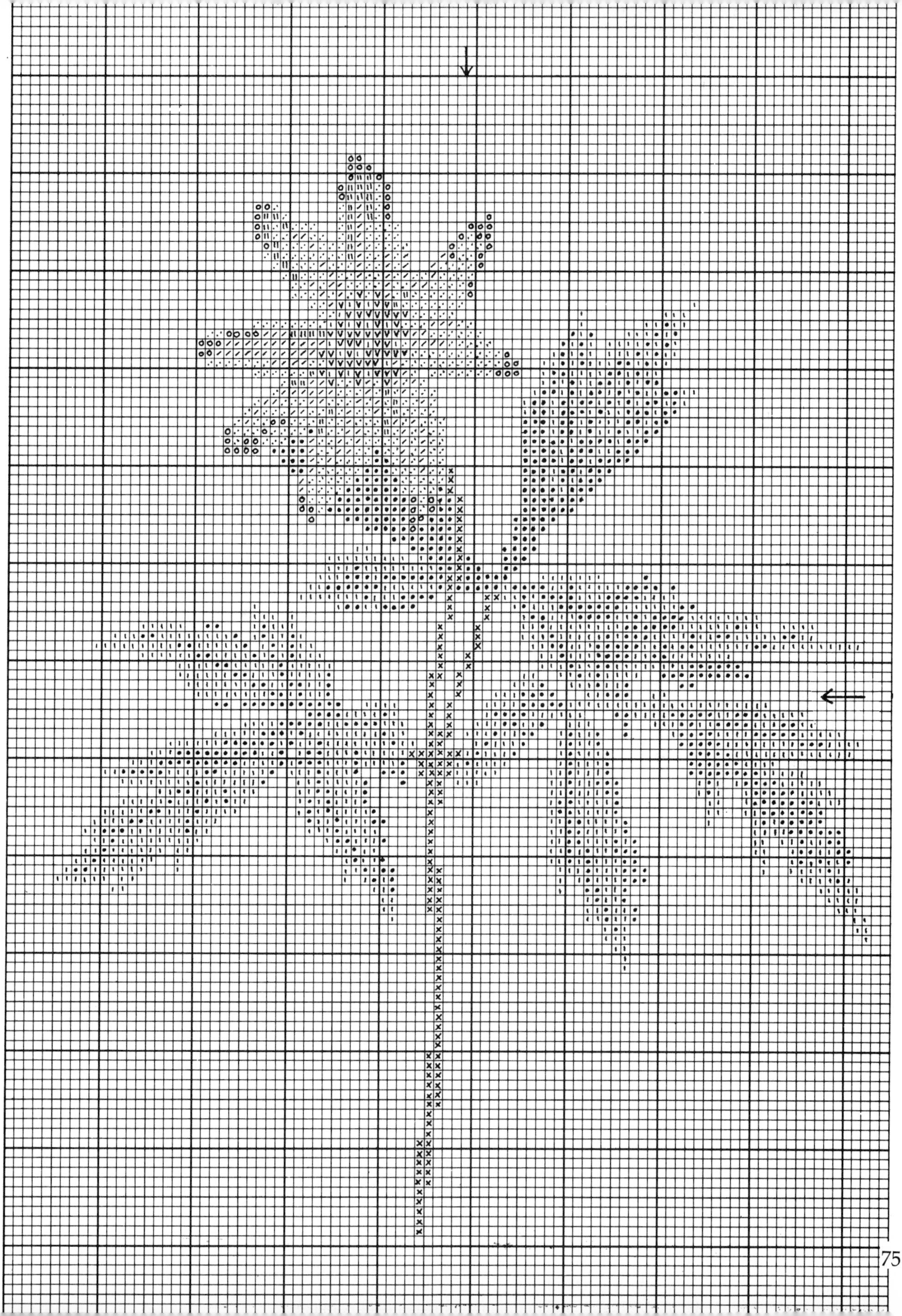

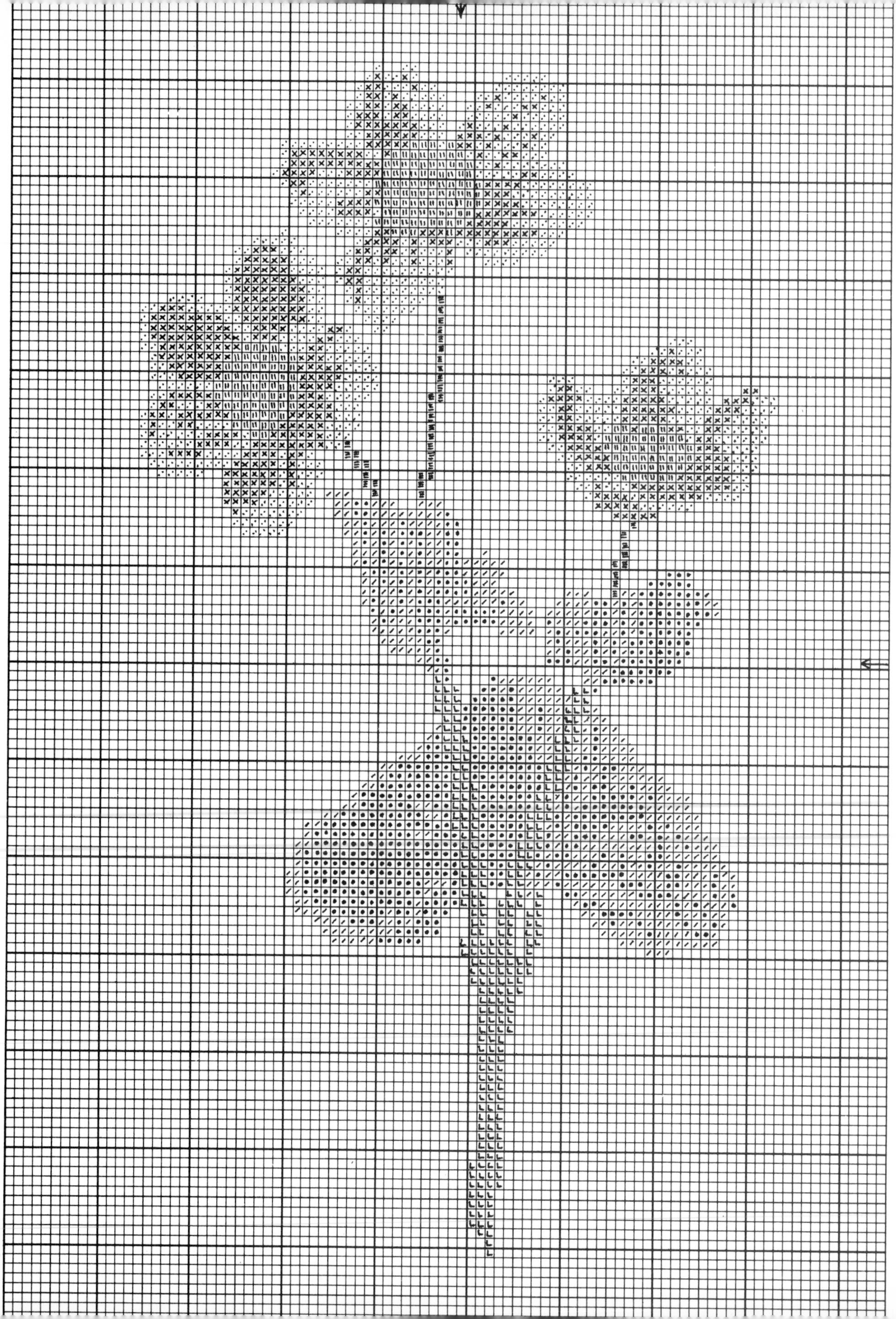

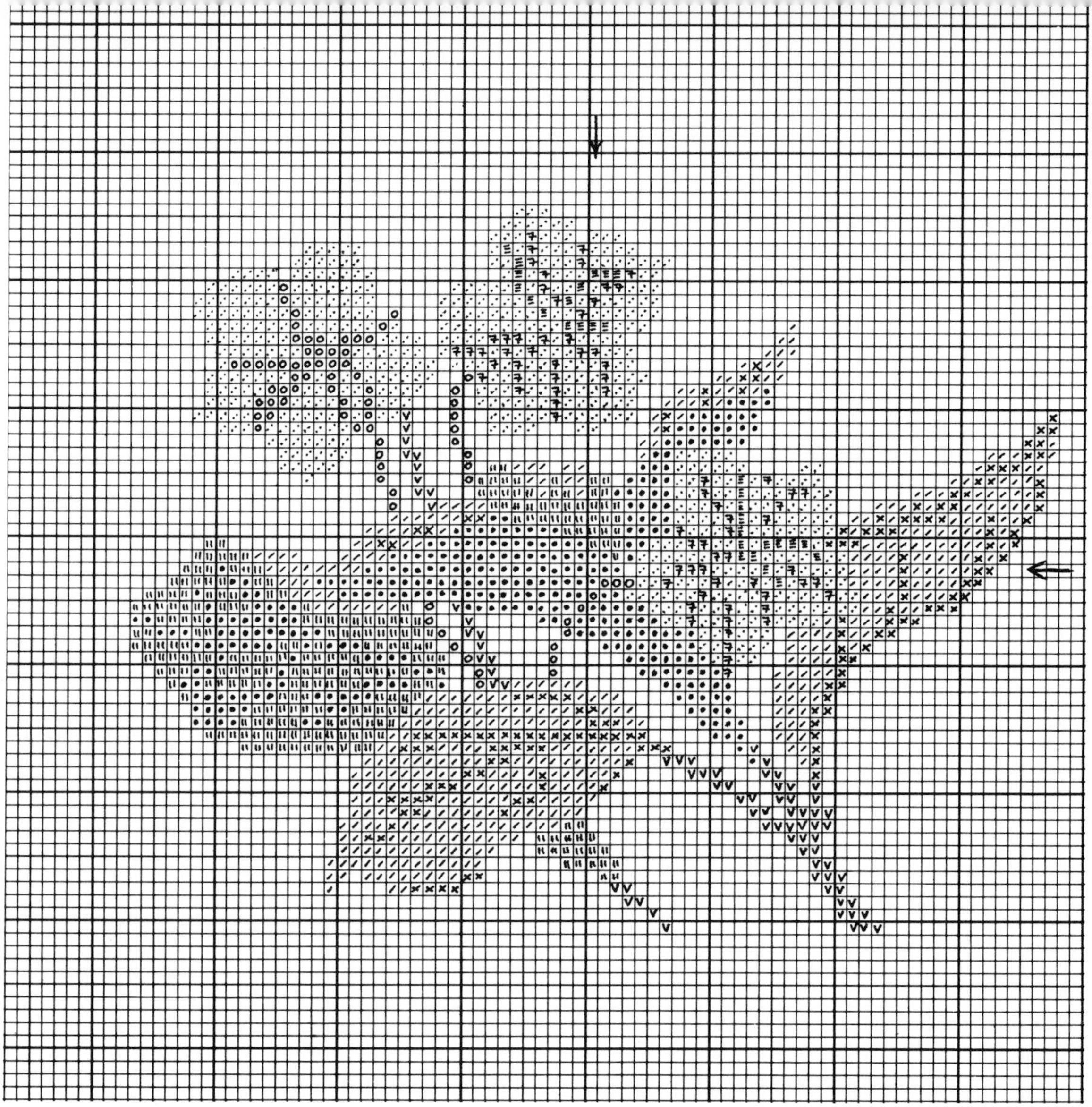

Marsh Marigold

⊡	742	Gold
☒	743	Deep Yellow
⁛	744	Yellow
☰	3347	Medium Yellow-Green
◿	368	Sage Green
⊙	3345	Forest Green
L	320	Pistachio Green

Wood Loosestrife

◿	368	Sage Green
☒	904	Dark Parrot Green
⁛	307	Bright Yellow
☰	444	Buttercup Yellow
≠	907	Light Green
V	3688	Light Mulberry
O	703	Chartreuse
⊙	3345	Forest Green
⊡	906	Parrot Green

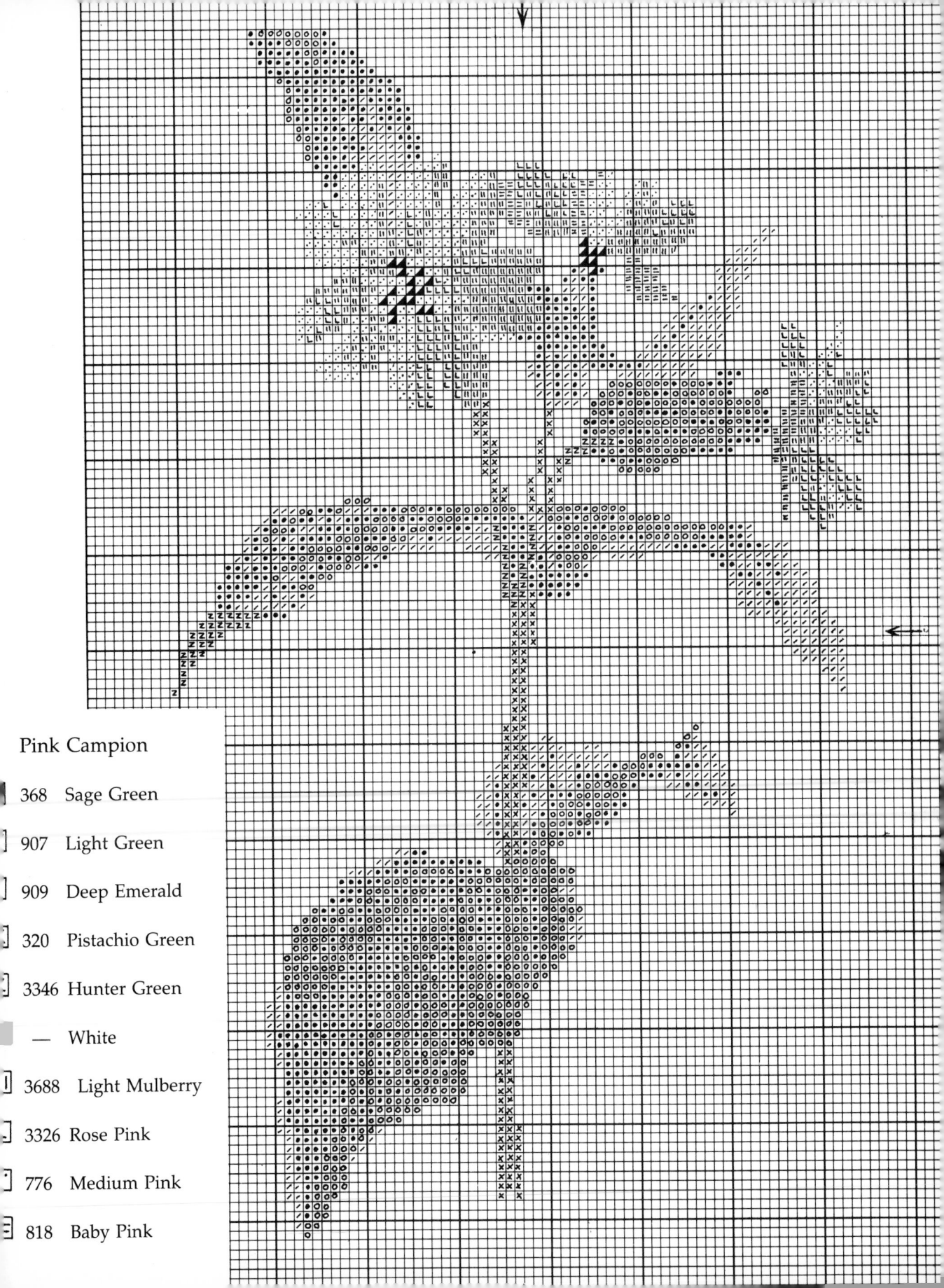

Pink Campion

Symbol	Code	Name
	368	Sage Green
	907	Light Green
	909	Deep Emerald
	320	Pistachio Green
	3346	Hunter Green
—		White
	3688	Light Mulberry
	3326	Rose Pink
	776	Medium Pink
	818	Baby Pink

Index of flowers